4th Workshop on Linked Data in Linguistics (LDL-2015)

Resources and Applications

Co-located with ACL-IJCNLP 2015

Beijing, China
31 July 2015

ISBN: 978-1-5108-0940-6

Printed from e-media with permission by:

Curran Associates, Inc.
57 Morehouse Lane
Red Hook, NY 12571

Some format issues inherent in the e-media version may also appear in this print version.

Printed by Curran Associates, Inc. (2015)

Association for Computational Linguistics
209 N. Eighth Street
Stroudsburg, Pennsylvania 18360

Phone: 1-570-476-8006
Fax: 1-570-476-0860

acl@aclweb.org

Additional copies of this publication are available from:

Curran Associates, Inc.
57 Morehouse Lane
Red Hook, NY 12571 USA
Phone: 845-758-0400
Fax: 845-758-2634
Email: curran@proceedings.com
Web: www.proceedings.com

ACL-IJCNLP 2015

The 53rd Annual Meeting of the Association for Computational Linguistics and the 7th International Joint Conference on Natural Language Processing

Proceedings of the 4th Workshop on Linked Data in Linguistics: Resources and Applications (LDL-2015)

July 31, 2015
Beijing, China

Linked Data in Linguistics 2015. Introduction and Overview

After half a century of computational linguistics, quantitative typology, empirical, corpus-based study of language, and computational lexicography, researchers in computational linguistics, natural language processing (NLP) or information technology as well as in digital humanities are confronted with an immense wealth of linguistic resources; and these are not only growing in number, but also in their heterogeneity. Accordingly, the limited interoperability between linguistic resources has been recognized as a major obstacle for data use and re-use within and across discipline boundaries, and represents one of the prime motivations for adopting linked data in our field.

With the rise of the Semantic Web, new representation formalisms and novel technologies have become available, and different communities are becoming increasingly aware of the potential of these developments with respect to the challenges posited by the heterogeneity and multitude of linguistic resources available today. Many of these approaches follow the **Linked (Open) Data paradigm**.

The LDL workshop series and LDL-2015 are organized by the Open Linguistics Working Group to bring together researchers from various fields of linguistics, NLP, and IT to present and discuss principles, case studies, and best practices for representing, publishing and linking linguistic data collections, and aims to facilitate the exchange of technologies, ideas and resources across discipline boundaries, that (to a certain extend) find a material manifestation in the emerging LLOD cloud.

LDL-2015, collocated with ACL-IJCNLP 2015, the 53rd Annual Meeting of the Association of Computational Linguistics and the 7th Joint Conference on Natural Language Processing of the Asian Federation of Natural Language Processing in July 2015 in Beijing, China, is the fourth workshop on Linked Data in Linguistics following LDL-2012 (March 2012 in Frankfurt am Main, Germany), LDL-2013 (Sep 2013 in Pisa, Italy), and LDL-2014 (May 2014, Reykjavik, Iceland), as well as more specialized events such as the workshops on Multilingual Linked Open Data for Enterprises (MLODE-2012: Sep 2012 in Leipzig, Germany, MLODE-2014: Sep 2014 in Leipzig, Germany), and Natural Language Processing and Linked Open Data (NLP&LOD-2013: Sep 2013 in Hissar, Bulgaria), and the theme session on Linked Data in Linguistic Typology (at the 10th Biennial Conference of the Association for Linguistic Typology, ALT-2013, Aug 2013 in Leipzig, Germany), as well as presentations, panels and informal meetings at various conferences.

LDL-2015 is organized by the *Open Linguistics Working Group* (OWLG) of the Open Knowledge Foundation and the **Ontology-Lexica Community (OntoLex) Group**[1]. Like LDL-2014, LDL-2015 is supported by the EU Projects LIDER and QTLeap: The project **Linked Data as an Enabler of Cross-Media and Multilingual Content Analytics for Enterprises Across Europe** (LIDER) aims to provide an ecosystem for the establishment of linguistic linked open data, as well as media resources metadata, for a free and open exploitation of such resources in multilingual, cross-media content analytics across Europe. The project **Quality Translation with Deep Language Engineering Approaches** (QTLeap) explores novel ways for attaining machine translation of higher quality that are opened by a new generation of increasingly sophisticated semantic datasets (including linked open data) and by recent advances in deep language processing.

For the 4th edition of the workshop on Linked Data in Linguistics, we invited contributions discussing the application of the Linked Open Data Paradigm to linguistic data in various fields of linguistics, natural language processing, knowledge management and information technology in order to present and discuss *principles*, *case studies*, and *best practices* for representing, publishing and linking mono- and multilingual linguistic and knowledge data collections, including corpora, grammars, dictionaries, wordnets, translation memories, domain specific ontologies etc.

[1] `http://www.w3.org/community/ontolex`

In this regard, the Linked Data Paradigm provides an important step towards making linguistic data: i) easily and uniformly queryable, ii) interoperable and iii) sharable over the Web using open standards such as the HTTP protocol and the RDF data model. As a result of preceding LDL workshops and the activities of the communities involved, a considerable amount of linguistic linked open data resources has been established, so that our community is now increasingly aiming to shift the focus from resource creation to resource linking and further to the development of innovative applications of these resources in linguistics and NLP. For the current issue of LDL, we thus focus on *resouces and applications*.

Accordingly, LDL-2015 provides a forum for researchers on natural language processing and semantic web technologies to present case studies and best practices on the exploitation of linguistic resources exposed on the Web for **natural language processing** applications, or other content-centered applications such as content analytics, knowledge extraction, etc. The availability of massive linked open knowledge resources raises the question how such data can be suitably employed to facilitate different NLP tasks and research questions. Following the tradition of earlier LDL workshops, we encouraged contributions to the Linguistic Linked Open Data (LLOD) cloud and research on this basis. In particular, this pertains to contributions that demonstrate an added value resulting from the combination of linked datasets and ontologies as a source for semantic information with linguistic resources published according to as linked data principles. Another important question to be addressed in the workshop is how natural language processing techniques can be employed to further facilitate the growth and enrichment of linguistic resources on the Web.

Invited Talk by Key-Sun Choi

In addition to full and short papers/dataset descriptions, LDL-2015 will feature Key-Sun Choi as an invited speaker. Key-Sun Choi is professor of the Korea Advanced Institute of Science and Technology (KAIST), Korea, since 1988, where he had been Head of Computer Science Department (2006-2011) and recently founded the KAIST research group on Open Knowledge Convergence (since 2012). Key-Sun Choi has contributed to Department of Knowledge Service Engineering and Graduate School of Information Security in KAIST as a Joint Professor.

He founded and directed Korterm (Korea Terminology Research Center for Natural Language and Knowledge Engineering, 1998) and Bora (National Research Resource Bank for Language and Annotation, 2003). He had been an invited researcher in NEC C&C Lab of Japan (1987-1988), a visiting scholar of CSLI of Stanford University (1997), and an invited researcher of NHK Science & Technology Research Laboratories (2002). His areas of expertise are natural language processing, ontology and knowledge engineering, semantic web and linked data, and their infrastructure including text analytics. He served as President (2009-2010) of AFNLP (Asia Federation of Natural Language Processing), the President (2006) of Korean Cognitive Science Society, and the Secretary of ISO/TC37/SC4 for language resource management standards since 2002.

Recent key areas of his work are entity linking and predicate linking from text to DBpedia-like knowledge-bases and the enrichment of text, mainly for Korean. In his talk, he will focus on this line of research and address aspects of lexicalizing ontologies, mapping local properties to ontologies, extracting base ontologies and enhancing multilingualism in DBpedia.

As organizers of LDL-2015, we are happy to welcome Key-Sun Choi as key note speaker to the workshop and look forward for fruitful discussions on the interface of Semantic Web and NLP in Beijing.

Organizers:

Christian Chiarcos, Goethe-Universität Frankfurt, Germany
Philipp Cimiano, Universität Bielefeld, Germany
Nancy Ide, Vassar College, NY
John P. McCrae, Universität Bielefeld, Germany
Petya Osenova, University of Sofia, Bulgaria

Program Committee:

Eneko Agirre, University of the Basque Country, Spain
Guadalupe Aguado, Universidad Politécnica de Madrid, Spain
Claire Bonial, University of Colorado at Boulder, USA
Peter Bouda, Interdisciplinary Centre for Social and Language Documentation, Portugal
Antonio Branco, University of Lisbon, Portugal
Martin Brümmer, University of Leipzig, Germany
Paul Buitelaar, INSIGHT, NUIG Galway, Ireland
Steve Cassidy, Macquarie University, Australia
Nicoletta Calzolari, ILC-CNR, Italy
Thierry Declerck, DFKI, Germany
Ernesto William De Luca, University of Applied Sciences Potsdam, Germany
Gerard de Melo, University of California at Berkeley
Judith Eckle-Kohler, Technische Universität Darmstadt, Germany
Francesca Frontini, ILC-CNR, Italy
Jeff Good, University at Buffalo
Asunción Gómez Pérez, Universidad Politécnica de Madrid
Jorge Gracia, Universidad Politécnica de Madrid, Spain
Walther v. Hahn, University of Hamburg, Germany
Yoshihiko Hayashi, Waseda University, Japan
Fahad Khan, ILC-CNR, Italy
Seiji Koide, National Institute of Informatics, Japan
Bettina Klimek, Universität Leipzig, Germany
Lutz Maicher, Universität Leipzig, Germany
Elena Montiel-Ponsoda, Universidad Politécnica de Madrid, Spain
Steven Moran, Universität Zürich, Switzerland/Ludwig Maximilian University, Germany
Sebastian Nordhoff, Max Planck Institute for Evolutionary Anthropology, Leipzig, Germany
Antonio Pareja-Lora, Universidad Complutense Madrid, Spain
Maciej Piasecki, Wroclaw University of Technology, Poland
Francesca Quattri (Hong Kong Polytechnic University, Hong Kong
Laurent Romary, INRIA, France
Felix Sasaki, Deutsches Forschungszentrum für Künstliche Intelligenz, Germany
Andrea Schalley, Griffith University, Australia
Gilles Sérraset, Joseph Fourier University, France
Kiril Simov, Bulgarian Academy of Sciences, Sofia, Bulgaria
Milena Slavcheva, JRC-Brussels, Belgium
Armando Stellato, University of Rome, Tor Vergata, Italy
Marco Tadic, University of Zagreb, Croatia
Marieke van Erp, VU University Amsterdam, The Netherlands

Daniel Vila, Universidad Politécnica de Madrid
Cristina Vertan, University of Hamburg, Germany
Menzo Windhouwer, Max Planck Institute for Psycholinguistics, Nijmegen, The Netherlands

Invited Speaker:

Key-Sun Choi, KAIST, Korea

Table of Contents

This page intentionally left blank.

Conference Program

9:00-9:30 Introduction

9:30-10:30 Invited Talk: "DBpedia and Mulitlingualism"
Key-Sun Choi

10:30-11:00 Coffee break

11:00-11:30 *From DBpedia and WordNet hierarchies to LinkedIn and Twitter*
Aonghus McGovern, Alexander O'Connor and Vincent Wade

11:30-12:00 *A Linked Data Model for Multimodal Sentiment and Emotion Analysis*
J. Fernando Sánchez-Rada, Carlos A. Iglesias and Ronald Gil

12:00-12:30 *Seeing is Correcting: curating lexical resources using social interfaces*
Livy Real, Fabricio Chalub, Valeria dePaiva, Claudia Freitas and Alexandre Rademaker

12:30-14:00 Lunch

14:00-14:30 *Sar-graphs: A Linked Linguistic Knowledge Resource Connecting Facts with Language*
Sebastian Krause, Leonhard Hennig, Aleksandra Gabryszak, Feiyu Xu and Hans Uszkoreit

14:30-15:00 *Reconciling Heterogeneous Descriptions of Language Resources*
John Philip McCrae, Philipp Cimiano, Victor Rodriguez-Doncel, Daniel Vila Suero, Jorge Gracia, Luca Matteis, Roberto Navigli, Andrejs Abele, Gabriela Vulcu and Paul Buitelaar

15:00-15:30 *RDF Representation of Licenses for Language Resources*
Víctor Rodriguez-Doncel and Penny Labropoulou

15:30-16:00 Coffee break

16:00-16:20 *Linking Four Heterogeneous Language Resources as Linked Data*
Benjamin Siemoneit, John Philip McCrae and Philipp Cimiano

16:20-16:40 *EVALution 1.0: an Evolving Semantic Dataset for Training and Evaluation of Distributional Semantic Models*
Enrico Santus, Frances Yung, Alessandro Lenci and Chu-Ren Huang

16:40-17:00 *Linguistic Linked Data in Chinese: The Case of Chinese Wordnet*
Chih-Yao LEE and Shu-Kai HSIEH

17:00-17:30 Coffee break

From DBpedia and WordNet hierarchies to LinkedIn and Twitter

Aonghus McGovern
ADAPT Centre
Trinity College Dublin
Dublin, Ireland
amcgover@scss.tcd.ie

Alexander O'Connor
ADAPT Centre
Trinity College Dublin
Dublin, Ireland
Alex.OConnor@scss.tcd.ie

Vincent Wade
ADAPT Centre
Trinity College Dublin
Dublin, Ireland
Vincent.Wade@cs.tcd.ie

Abstract

Previous research has demonstrated the benefits of using linguistic resources to analyze a user's social media profiles in order to learn information about that user. However, numerous linguistic resources exist, raising the question of choosing the appropriate resource. This paper compares Extended WordNet Domains with DBpedia. The comparison takes the form of an investigation of the relationship between users' descriptions of their knowledge and background on LinkedIn with their description of the same characteristics on Twitter. The analysis applied in this study consists of four parts. First, information a user has shared on each service is mined for keywords. These keywords are then linked with terms in DBpedia/Extended WordNet Domains. These terms are ranked in order to generate separate representations of the user's interests and knowledge for LinkedIn and Twitter. Finally, the relationship between these separate representations is examined. In a user study with eight participants, the performance of this analysis using DBpedia is compared with the performance of this analysis using Extended WordNet Domains. The best results were obtained when DBpedia was used.

1 Introduction

Natural Language Processing (NLP) techniques have been shown in studies such as Gao et al. (2012) and Vosecky et al. (2013) to be successful in extracting information from a user's social media profiles. In these studies, linguistic resources are employed in order to perform NLP tasks such as identifying concepts, Named Entity Recognition etc. However, as Chiarcos et al. argue, significant interoperability issues are posed by the fact that linguistic resources 'are not only growing in number, but also in their heterogeneity' (2014). They further argue that the best way to overcome these issues is by using linguistic resources that conform to Linked Open Data principles. Chiarcos et al. divide such resources into two categories, distinguishing between strictly lexical resources such as WordNet and general knowledge bases such as DBpedia.

The study described in this paper examines a single resource of each type. WordNet is considered to be a representative example of a purely lexical resource given the extent of its use in research[1]. DBpedia is considered to be a representative example of a knowledge base because its information is derived from Wikipedia, the quality of whose knowledge almost matches that of Encyclopedia Britannica (Giles, 2005). These resources are compared by means of an investigation of the relationship between users' descriptions of their knowledge and background on LinkedIn with their description of the same characteristics on Twitter.

Both LinkedIn and Twitter allow users to describe their interests and knowledge by: (i) Filling in profile information (ii) Posting status updates. However, the percentage of users who post status updates on LinkedIn is significantly lower than the percentage of users who do so on Twitter (Bullas, 2015). On the other hand, LinkedIn users fill in far more of their profiles on average than Twitter users (Abel, Henze, Herder, and Krause, 2010).

[1] A list of publications involving WordNet: http://lit.csci.unt.edu/~wordnet/

Proceedings of the 4th Workshop on Linked Data in Linguistics (LDL-2015), pages 1–10,
Beijing, China, July 31, 2015. ©2015 Association for Computational Linguistics and Asian Federation of Natural Language Processing

Given the different ways in which users use these services, it is possible that they provide different representations of their interests and knowledge on each one. For example, a user may indicate a new-found interest in 'Linguistics' through their tweets before they list this subject on their LinkedIn profile. This study examines the relationship between users' descriptions of their interests and knowledge on each service.

2 Related Work

Hauff and Houben describe a study that investigates whether a user's bookmarking profile on the sites Bibsonomy, CiteULike and LibraryThing can be inferred using information obtained from that user's tweets (2011) . Hauff and Houben generate separate 'knowledge profiles' for Twitter and for the bookmarking sites. These profiles consist of a weighted list of terms that appear in the user's tweets and bookmarking profiles, respectively. The authors' approach is hindered by noise introduced by tweets that are unrelated to the user's learning activities. This problem could be addressed by enriching information found in a user's profiles with structured data in a linguistic resource.

However, there are often multiple possible interpretations for a term. For example, the word 'bank' has entirely different interpretations when it appears to the right of the word 'river' than when it appears to the right of the word 'merchant'. When linking a word with information contained in a linguistic resource, the correct interpretation of the word must be chosen. The NLP technique Word Sense Disambiguation (WSD) addresses this issue. Two different approaches to WSD are described below.

Magnini et al. perform WSD using WordNet as well as domain labels provided by the WordNet Domains project[2] (2002). This project assigned domain labels to WordNet synsets in accordance with the Dewey Decimal Classification. However, WordNet has been updated with new synsets since Magnini et al.'s study. Therefore, in the study described in this paper, the Extended WordNet Domain labels created by González et al. (2012) are used. Not only do these labels provide greater synset coverage, González et al. report better WSD performance with Extended WordNet Domains than with the original WordNet Domains.

Mihalcea and Csomai describe an approach for identifying the relevant Wikipedia articles for a piece of text (2007). Their approach employs a combination of the Lesk algorithm and Naïve Bayes classification. Since DBpedia URIs are created using Wikipedia article titles, the above approach can also be used to identify DBpedia entities in text.

Magnini et al's approach offers a means of analysing the skill, interest and course lists on a user's LinkedIn profile with regard to both WordNet and DBpedia. Unambiguous items in these lists can be linked directly with a WordNet synset or DBpedia URI. These unambiguous items can then provide a basis for interpreting ambiguous terms. For example, the unambiguous 'XML' could be linked with the 'Computer Science' domain, providing a basis for interpreting the ambiguous 'Java'.

The above analysis allows for items in a user's tweets and LinkedIn profile to be linked with entities in WordNet/DBpedia. Labels associated with these entities can then be collected to form separate term-list representations for a user's tweets and LinkedIn profile information.

Plumbaum et al. describe a Social Web User Model as consisting of the following attributes: Personal Characteristics, Interests, Knowledge and Behavior, Needs and Goals and Context (2011). Inferring 'Personal Characteristics' (i.e. demographic information) from either a user's tweets or their LinkedIn profile information would require a very different kind of analysis from that described in this paper, for example that performed by Schler and Koppel (2006). As Plumbaum et al. define 'Behaviour' and 'Needs and Goals' as system-specific characteristics, information about a specific system would be

[2] http://wndomains.fbk.eu/

required to infer them. 'Context' requires information such as the user's role in their social network to be inferred.

Given the facts stated in the previous paragraph, the term lists generated by the analysis in this study are taken as not describing 'Personal Characteristics', 'Behavior', 'Needs and Goals' and 'Context'. However, a term-list format has been used to represent interests and knowledge by Ma, Zeng, Ren, and Zhong (2011) and Hauff and Houben (2011), respectively. As mentioned previously, users' Twitter and LinkedIn profiles can contain information about both characteristics. Thus, the term lists generated in this study are taken as representing a combination of the user's interests and knowledge.

3 Research Questions

3.1 Research Question 1

This question investigates the possibility that a user may represent their interests and knowledge differently on different Social Media services. It is as follows:

RQ1. *To what extent does a user's description of their interests and knowledge through their tweets correspond with their description of the same characteristics through their profile information on LinkedIn?*

For example, 'Linguistics' may be the most discussed item in the user's LinkedIn profile, but only the third most discussed item in their tweets.

This question is similar to that investigated by Hauff and Houben (2011). However, there is an important difference. This question does not try to determine whether a user's LinkedIn profile can be inferred from their tweets. Instead, it investigates the extent of the difference between the information users give through each service.

3.2 Research Question 2

Studies such as Abel et al. (2011; 2012) show that information found in a user's tweets can be used to recommend items to them e.g. news articles. Furthermore, as user activity is significantly higher on Twitter than on LinkedIn (Bullas, 2015), users may discuss recent interests on the former without updating the latter. The second research question of this study is as follows:

RQ2. *Can information obtained from a user's tweets be used to recommend items for that user's LinkedIn page?*

These questions aim to investigate: (i) The variation between a user's description of their interests and knowledge through their LinkedIn profile and their description of these characteristics through their tweets (ii) Whether a user's tweets can be used to augment the information in their LinkedIn profile.

4 Method

The user study method is applied in this research. This decision is taken with reference to work such as Lee and Brusilovsky (2009) and Reinecke and Bernstein (2009). The aforementioned authors employ user studies in order to determine the accuracy with which their systems infer information about users.

4.1 Analysis

The analysis adopted in this study consists of four stages:

- Identify keywords
- Link these keywords to labels in DBpedia /Extended WordNet Domains)
- Generate separate representations of the user's interests and knowledge for their tweets and LinkedIn profile information
- Examine the relationship between these separate representations

4.2 Keyword Identification

The user's LinkedIn lists of skills, interests and courses are treated as lists of keywords with respect to each resource. However, the process for identifying keywords in text (e.g. a textual description on LinkedIn, a tweet) differs for each resource. For the DBpedia approach potential keywords derive from a precompiled list i.e. the list of all Wikipedia keyphrases. In the case of Extended WordNet Domains, no such list exists, meaning a different approach must be used for identifying keywords. Ellen Riloff describes various methods for identifying important items in a text (1999). Riloff describes how case frames can be used to identify nouns describing entities such as perpetrators and victims of crimes. A case frame approach cannot be adopted here as it relies on previous knowledge of the text being processed. Instead, each text is parsed in order to extract its noun phrases. These noun phrases are then investigated using n-grams for keywords that can be linked with WordNet synsets.

Keywords relating to Named Entities of the following types are ignored: Person; Place; Organization; Event; Animal; Film; Television Show; Book; Play (Theatre). This is because in a list of top LinkedIn skills compiled by *LinkedIn Profile Services*[3], not a single Named Entity of these types appears.

Any links appearing in text are extracted and cleaned of HTML. The remaining text is analysed in the manner detailed in the two previous paragraphs.

4.3 Linking keywords with labels

Ma et al. discuss methods for identifying user interests by combining information from different sources, including LinkedIn and Twitter (2011). The authors argue that, with the help of domain ontologies, texts a user has written can be used to identify both explicit and implicit interests. Explicit interests are identified by linking text items with ontology classes. Implicit interests are then identified by obtaining the parent and/or child of the identified ontology class. For example, consider an ontology in which 'Knowledge Representation' is the parent of 'Semantic Web'. If a user explicitly indicates they are interested in 'Semantic Web', they are implicitly indicating that they are interested in 'Knowledge Representation'. However, Ma et al. provide the caveat that only the immediate parents and children of a particular class (i.e. one level above/below) should be identified for a particular class.

In the study described in this paper, explicit information is obtained by linking keywords with labels in DBpedia/Extended WordNet Domains. Unambiguous keywords are linked directly. Ambiguous keywords are linked to labels using the methods described in the 'Related Work' section. Implicit information is obtained by identifying parent class(es) only. This decision was taken with reference to the 'is-a' subsumption relation. Under this relation, if an object B inherits from an object A, all instances of B are instances of A. However, instances of A are not necessarily instances of B. For example, if a user explicitly expresses an interest in 'Knowledge Representation' they are not necessarily implicitly expressing an interest in 'Semantic Web'.

4.4 Representation of user interests and knowledge

User interests and knowledge are represented as weighted lists of terms. Weighting schemes such as tf-idf are not used because as Hauff and Houben argue, such measures are not best suited to measuring the relative importance of terms for a user. The authors describe the inherent problem with measures such as tf-idf: 'if a tenth of the CiteULike articles in our index for example would include the term genetics, it would receive a low weight, although it may actually represent the user's knowledge profile very well' (2011). The procedure for calculating term weights in this study is thus identical to that in Hauff and Houben's study. A term's weight is calculated using the following formula:

$$weight = \frac{\text{number of times term was mentioned}}{\text{total number of term mentions}}$$

[3] Available at: http://linkedinprofileservice.co/linkedin-profile-tips-advice/linkedin-skills-list/

For example, if there are a total of 4 term mentions and 'Linguistics' has been mentioned twice its weight will be 0.5.

Terms with only a single mention are discarded before weights are calculated. This decision was taken in order to minimise noise in the form of outlying items.

4.5 Comparison of representations

A term's weight in the LinkedIn or Twitter term lists generated by this analysis is directly related to the total number of term mentions in that list. As this total can differ between LinkedIn and Twitter, comparisons between term lists cannot be made using weights. Ranks are used instead.

For RQ1 the relative ranks of terms that appear in both the Twitter and LinkedIn term lists are compared.

For RQ2, only Twitter terms whose rank is equal to or higher than the lowest ranked term in the LinkedIn term list are recommended. For example, if the user's LinkedIn term list contains six ranks, only Twitter terms of rank six or higher are recommended. If no terms were found in the user's LinkedIn profile, only the first-ranked Twitter interest(s) is recommended.

5 Implementation

This section describes the implementation of the analysis described in the previous section.

5.1 Information Collected

The user's 1000 most recent tweets are collected using Twitter's public RESTful API[4]. The following information is collected using LinkedIn's public RESTful API[5]:

1. The user's summary
2. The user's skill, interest and course lists
3. The user's textual descriptions of their educational and professional experience.
4. The textual descriptions of LinkedIn groups to which the user belongs.

[4] https://dev.twitter.com/rest/public

[5] https://developer.linkedin.com/docs/rest-api

5.2 Term selection from resources

In WordNet, the hyperonymy relation links a noun synset to its parent. Analogously to the Swedish FrameNet++ lexical framework described by Forsberg and Borin (2014), in this study the Simple Knowledge Organization System (SKOS)[6] 'broader' relation is used as a DBpedia equivalent to hyperonymy.

5.2.1 WordNet

Extended WordNet Domain labels are used as terms. A keyword is linked to a WordNet synset and the domain label for this synset as well as the domain labels for its hyperonyms are obtained.

The '*factotum*' domain is not considered. This label is assigned to synsets to which no other label could be assigned, and thus has no specificity.

5.2.2 DBpedia

DBpedia category labels are used as terms. A keyword is linked to a DBpedia URI. This URI is then linked to the DBpedia category bearing the same label using the Dublin Core[7] 'subject' relation. If no such category exists, this means this URI content did not meet the criteria required to be given its own category[8]. In this case, all categories related to the URI by the 'subject' relation are obtained. Parent categories are identified through the SKOS 'broader' relation, and their labels are obtained.

The DBpedia category 'Main topic classifications' is not considered as it is a table of contents for other categories. Similarly, DBpedia categories such as 'Wikipedia categories named after information technology companies of the United States' are not considered as these refer specifically to the way in which the Wikipedia hierarchy is organised, rather than the concepts in it.

[6] http://www.w3.org/2004/02/skos/

[7] http://dublincore.org/

[8] Guidelines for creating Wikipedia categories: http://en.wikipedia.org/wiki/Wikipedia:Categorization

5.3 Texts

Texts (i.e. tweets, LinkedIn descriptions) are parsed, and the WordNet and DBpedia databases accessed, using the Pattern NLP library for Python (Smedt & Daelemans, 2012).

5.3.1 Tweet Preprocessing

Before tweets are analysed, they are preprocessed as follows:

- The word 'RT' appearing at the beginning of a tweet (indicating the tweet is a retweet) is removed.
- Characters repeated consecutively more than twice are replaced with two consecutive characters (e.g. 'gooood' becomes become 'good') as in (Vosecky et al., 2013).
- For hashtags the '#' symbol is removed and the tag is split using the capital-letter rule described in (Hauff & Houben, 2011). For example, '#MachineLearning' becomes 'Machine Learning'.

5.3.2 Corpora Used

In applying Magnini et al's approach, separate corpora are used for processing tweets and for processing LinkedIn textual data. For the former, a 36.4 million-word tweet corpus is used. For the latter the ~300 million-word blog corpus compiled by Schler and Koppel (2006) is used. This corpus is deemed suitable given both its size and the fact that it contains posts on a wide variety of topics, for example: 'Real Estate', 'Arts', 'Education', 'Engineering', 'Law' etc.

5.3.3 Modifications

This section describes modifications made to the analysis described in the 'Method' Section.

Magnini et al report that a context of at least 100 words should be used to disambiguate a word (50 words before the word and 50 words after). For tweets, as such a context is not available, the whole tweet is used.

The following modifications were made due to analysis time constraints.

Only links of 550 words or lower were analysed. This decision was taken with reference to the following quote from a Reuters blog post on the issue of ideal article length: 'Reuters editors see stories that exceed 500 or 600 words as indistinguishable from "Gravity's Rainbow")' (MacMillan, 2010).

In the DBpedia approach, creating feature vectors for the Naïve Bayes approach proved unworkable. Consider for example the term 'Xbox', which appears as a keyphrase in 4008 articles. To apply the Naïve Bayes approach, the following information would have to be gathered for each occurrence: 'the current word and its part-of-speech, a local context of three words to the left and right of the ambiguous word, the parts-of-speech of the surrounding words, and a global context implemented through sense specific keywords determined as a list of at most five words occurring at least three times in the contexts defining a certain word sense.'(Mihalcea and Csomai, 2007). This proved to be prohibitively expensive in terms of time taken. Thus, only Lesk's algorithm is used to disambiguate keywords in the DBpedia approach. However, the results reported by Mihalcea and Csomai for WSD using Lesk's algorithm alone are higher than approaches such as Agirre and Soroa (2009) and Gomes et al (2003). Thus, disambiguation quality is preserved.

6 Evaluation

Eight users participated in the evaluation. Participants were identified by two means: An email circulated in the research group in which the authors work; Tweeting at Twitter users from the university in which the authors work

The study is split into two sessions. In the first session, the user logs in to their Twitter and LinkedIn accounts. Their data is then collected and analysis performed. In the second session, the user is asked to subjectively evaluate DBpedia and Extended WordNet Domains with regard to each research question.

It must be noted that the number of participants in this experiment was quite small. As such, it would be unwise to make strong inferences from the results reported below.

6.1 RQ1 Procedure

Term comparisons are represented similarly to the study performed by Holland et al. (2003). Holland et al. represent user preferences for particular products in the format 'A is better than B'.

For RQ1, the user is shown a series of assertions about the relative ranks of terms that appear in both their Twitter and LinkedIn term lists. For example, if 'Linguistics' is the third ranked term in the user's LinkedIn term list but the fifth ranked term in their Twitter term list, the user is shown a statement asserting that Linguistics has less prominence in their tweets than in their LinkedIn profile. The user can answer affirmatively or negatively to each assertion. However, if the analysis has incorrectly identified a term, the user can indicate this instead of responding. They can also indicate that the term denotes an area that was of interest to them, but is not anymore.

If a term appears in the user's LinkedIn term list but not in their Twitter term list, the user is shown a statement asserting that the term has less prominence in their tweets than in their LinkedIn profile. If the user's LinkedIn term list is empty - as occurred with one user whose LinkedIn profile was sparse – no comparisons are made.

6.2 RQ2 Procedure

The approach for this question is similar to that adopted by Lee and Brusilovsky (2009). Lee and Brusilovsky use user judgments to evaluate the quality of the recommendations generated by their system. However, in Lee and Brusilovksy's study a Likert scale is used whereas in this study a multiple- choice format is used.

The user is shown a series of recommendations for their LinkedIn profile. The user can answer affirmatively or negatively to each recommendation. Alternatively, they can indicate that although the term denotes an area of interest to them they would not add it to their LinkedIn profile. This could be because they do not want to list the term on their professional profile or they do not feel sufficiently confident in their knowledge of the subject the term denotes. They can also indicate that the term denotes an area that was of interest to them, but is not anymore.

For the DBpedia approach, terms in the format 'Branches of X' are presented to the user as 'X', as these pages contain lists of sub-disciplines. For example, 'Branches of Psychology' becomes 'Psychology'. Similarly, terms in the format 'X by issue' are presented to the user as 'X'.

A user score is calculated for each lexical resource, with each research question contributing 50%. The scores from each user are then aggregated to give a final score for each resource.

7 Results

Table 1 illustrates the scores for each research question, while Table 2 shows error values. Extended WordNet Domains and DBpedia Categories are denoted using the acronyms EWND and DBC respectively. The figures in the tables are rounded.

Table Descriptions

Table 1

- ScrRQ1 – RQ1 score. The ratio of the number of correct comparisons to the total number of comparisons made.
- ScrRQ2 – RQ2 score. The ratio of the number of correct recommendations to the total number of recommendations made.

	ScrRQ1	ScrRQ2	Total	Total (all recs.)
EWND	40	30	35	54
DBC	62	51	53	70

Table 1. RQ1 and RQ2 Score percentages

	RQ1TermErr	ErrRQ2	RQ1Past	RQ2Past
EWND	29	30	4	1
DBC	16	14	0	0

Table 2. Error rate percentages

- Total – Obtained by adding the previous two scores together and dividing by 2.
- Total (all recs.) – The total including recommendations that were correct but which the user would not add to their LinkedIn profile.

Table 2

- Rq1TermErr – The percentage of prominence comparisons made containing incorrectly identified terms.
- ErrRQ2 – The percentage of incorrectly recommended terms.
- RQ1Past – The percentage of prominence comparisons made containing past interests.
- RQ2Past – The percentage of recommendations made containing past interests.

8 Discussion

The Extended WordNet Domains approach shows almost twice the percentage of incorrectly identified terms than the DBpedia approach. It also shows more than twice the percentage of incorrect recommendations. A reason for this can be found by examining the Extended WordNet Domains hierarchy. For example, consider the word 'law'. One of the possible synsets for this word defines it as 'the collection of rules imposed by authority'. The domain label for this synset is 'law'. The hyperonym for this synset is 'collection' whose definition is 'several things grouped together or considered as a whole'. The domain label for this synset is 'philately'. This directly contradicts the original WordNet Domains hierarchy, in which 'law' is a subclass of 'social science'.

The small number of study participants notwithstanding, the low error figures in the DBpedia approach look promising with regard to the task of profile aggregation. Abel et al. find that 'Profile aggregation provides multi-faceted profiles that reveal significantly more information about the users than individual service profiles can provide' (2010). Thus, a method that can accurately compare and combine information from a user's different profiles has value.

The marked difference between the 'Total' and 'Total (all recs.)' columns in Table 1 is also noteworthy. This indicates that there are certain subjects the study participants intended for Twitter, but not for LinkedIn.

One aspect of this study in need of improvement is the prominence comparisons (RQ1). During this part of the experiment, some participants said that they could not be sure about the relative weights of individual subject areas in their tweets and LinkedIn profile. However, in this case users were instructed to answer negatively so as not to artificially inflate scores. One way of overcoming this problem could be to generate ranked term lists for each profile and ask the user to subjectively evaluate each list separately.

9 Conclusion

This paper described a comparison between the Extended WordNet Domains and DBpedia lexical resources. The comparison took the form of an investigation of the ways in which users represent their interests and knowledge through their LinkedIn profile with the way they represent these characteristics through their tweets. In a user study with 8 participants the DBpedia category labels performed better than the WordNet Domain labels with regard to both research questions investigated.

10 Credits

This research is supported by the Science Foundation Ireland (Grant 07/CE/I1142) in the ADAPT Centre (www.adaptcentre.ie) at Trinity College, Dublin.

11 References

Fabian Abel, Nicola Henze, Eelco Herder and Daniel Krause. (2010). Interweaving public user profiles on the web. *User Modeling, Adaptation, and Personalization*, pp. 16–27.

Fabian Abel, Eelco Herder, Geert-Jan Houben, Nicola Henze, and Daniel Krause (2012). Cross-system user modeling and personalization on the Social Web. *User Modeling and User-Adapted Interaction*, pp. 169–209.

Eneko Agirre, and Aitor Soroa. (2009). Personalizing pagerank for word sense disambiguation. *Proceedings of the 12th Conference of the European Chapter of the Association for Computational Linguistics*, pp. 33–41.

Lars Borin and Markus Forsberg. (2014). Swesaurus, or The Frankenstein Approach to Wordnet Construction. *Proceedings of the Seventh Global Wordnet Conference*, pp. 215–223.

Jeff Bullas. (2015). *5 insights into the Latest Social Media Facts, Figures and Statistics*. [Online] Available at: http://www.jeffbullas.com/2013/07/04/5-insights-into-the-latest-social-media-facts-figures-and-statistics/. [Accessed 25 March 2015]

Christian Chiarcos, John Mccrae, Petya Osenova, and Cristina Vertan. (2014). Linked Data in Linguistics 2014 . Introduction and Overview. *3rd Workshop on Linked Data in Linguistics: Multilingual Knowledge Resources and Natural Language Processing*, pp. vii–xv.

Qi Gao, Fabian Abel and Geert-Jan Houben. (2012). GeniUS: generic user modeling library for the social semantic web. *Proceedings of the Joint International Semantic Technology Conference*, pp. 160–175.

Jim Giles. (2005). Internet encyclopaedias go head to head. *Nature*, Vol. 438, pp. 900–901.

Paulo Gomes, Francisco C. Pereira, Paulo Paiva, Nuno Seco, Paulo Carreiro, José Luís Ferreira., and Carlos Bento. (2003). Noun sense disambiguation with WordNet for software design retrieval. 16th Conference of the Canadian Society for Computational Studies of Intelligence, pp. 537–543.

Aitor González, German Rigau, and Mauro Castillo. (2012). A graph-based method to improve WordNet Domains. *Proceedings of the Computational Linguistics and Intelligent Text Processing Conference*, pp.17–28.

Claudia Hauff, and Geert-Jan Houben. (2011). Deriving Knowledge Profiles from Twitter. *Proceedings of 6th European Conference on Technology Enhanced Learning: Towards Ubiquitous Learning*, pp. 139–152.

Danielle H. Lee, Peter Brusilovsky. (2009). Reinforcing Recommendation Using Negative Feedback. *User Modeling, Adaptation, and Personalization*, pp. 422–427.

Yunfei Ma, Yi Zeng, Xu Ren, and Ning Zhong. (2011). User interests modeling based on multi-source personal information fusion and semantic reasoning. *Proceedings of theActive Media Technology Conference*, pp. 195–205.

Robert MacMillan. (2010). *Michael Kinsley and the length of newspaper articles*.[Online] Available at: http://blogs.reuters.com/mediafile/2010/01/05/michael-kinsley-and-the-length-of-newspaper-articles/. [Accessed 13 March 2015].

Bernardo Magnini, Carlo Strapparava, Giovanni Pezzulo, and Alfio Massimiliano Gliozzo. (2002). The role of domain information in word sense disambiguation. *Natural Language Engineering*, vol. 8, pp. 359 – 373.

Rada Mihalcea, and Andras Csomai. (2007). Wikify!: linking documents to encyclopedic knowledge. *Proceedings of the Sixteenth ACM Conference on Conference on Information and Knowledge Management*. pp. 233-242.

Till Plumbaum, Songxuan Wu, Ernesto William De Luca and Sahin Albayrak (2011). User Modeling for the Social Semantic Web. *Workshop on Semantic Personalized Information Management*, pp. 78–89.

Katharina Reinecke and Abraham Bernstein:. (2009). Tell Me Where You ' ve Lived , and I ' ll Tell You What You Like : Adapting Interfaces to Cultural Preferences. *User Modeling, Adaptation, and Personalization*, pp. 185–196.

Ellen Riloff. (1999). Information Extraction as a Stepping Stone toward Story Understanding. *Understanding Language Understanding: Computational Models of Reading*, pp. 1–24.

Jonathan Schler, Moshe Koppel, Shlomo Argamon and James W. Pennebaker. (2006). Effects of Age and Gender on Blogging. *Proceedings of AAAI Spring Symposium on Computational Approaches for Analyzing Weblogs*. pp. 199-205

Tom De Smedt and Walter Daelemans. (2012). Pattern for Python. *Journal of Machine Learning Research*, vol. 13, pp. 2063–2067.

Jan Vosecky, Di Jiang, Kenneth Wai-Ting Leung and Wilfred Ng. (2013). Dynamic Multi-Faceted Topic Discovery in Twitter. *Proceedings of the 22nd ACM International Conference on Information & Knowledge Management*, pp. 879–884.

A Linked Data Model for Multimodal Sentiment and Emotion Analysis

J. Fernando Sánchez-Rada
Grupo de Sistemas Inteligentes
Universidad Politécnica de Madrid
`jfernando@dit.upm.es`

Carlos A. Iglesias
Grupo de Sistemas Inteligentes
Universidad Politécnica de Madrid
`cif@dit.upm.es`

Ronald Gil
Massachusetts Institute of Technology
`rongil@mit.edu`

Abstract

The number of tools and services for sentiment analysis is increasing rapidly. Unfortunately, the lack of standard formats hinders interoperability. To tackle this problem, previous works propose the use of the NLP Interchange Format (NIF) as both a common semantic format and an API for textual sentiment analysis. However, that approach creates a gap between textual and sentiment analysis that hampers multimodality. This paper presents a multimedia extension of NIF that can be leveraged for multimodal applications. The application of this extended model is illustrated with a service that annotates online videos with their sentiment and the use of SPARQL to retrieve results for different modes.

1 Introduction

With the rise of social media and crowdsourcing, the interest in automatic means of extraction and aggregation of user opinions (Opinion Mining) and emotions (Emotion Mining) is growing. This tendency is mainly focused on text analysis, the cause and consequence of this being that the tools for text analysis are getting better and more accurate. As is often the case, these tools are heterogeneous and implement different formats and APIs. This problem is hardly new or limited to sentiment analysis, it is also present in the Natural Language Processing (NLP) field. In fact, both fields are closely related: textual sentiment analysis can be considered a branch of NLP. Looking at how NLP deals with heterogeneity and interoperability we find NIF, a format for NLP services that solves these issues. Unfortunately, *NLP Interchange Format* (NIF) (Hellmann et al., 2013) is not enough to annotate sentiment analysis services. Fortunately, it can be extended, by exploiting the extensibility of semantic formats. Using this extensibility and already existing ontologies for the sentiment and emotion domains, the R&D Eurosentiment project recently released a model that extends NIF for sentiment analysis (Buitelaar et al., 2013).

However, the Eurosentiment model is bound to textual sentiment analysis, as NIF focuses on annotation of text. The R&D MixedEmotions project aims at bridging this gap by providing a Big Linked Data Platform for multimedia and multilingual sentiment and emotion analysis. Hence, different modes (e.g. images, video, audio) require different formats. Format heterogeneity becomes problematic when different modes coexist or when the text is part of other media. Some examples of this include working with text extracted from a picture with OCR, or subtitles and transcripts of audio and video. This scenario is not uncommon, given the maturity of textual sentiment analysis tools.

In particular, this paper focuses on video and audio sources that contain emotions and opinions, such as public speeches. We aim to represent that information in a linked data format, linking the original source with its transcription and any sentiments or emotions found in any of its modes. Using the new model it is possible to represent and process multimodal sentiment information using a common set of tools.

The rest of the paper is structured as follows: Section 2 covers the background for this work; Section 3 presents requirements for semantic annotation of sentiment in multimedia; Section 4

Proceedings of the 4th Workshop on Linked Data in Linguistics (LDL-2015), pages 11–19,
Beijing, China, July 31, 2015.

introduces the bases for sentiment analysis using NIF and delves into the use of NIF for media other than text; Section 5 exemplifies the actual application of the new model with a prototype and semantic queries; Section 6 is dedicated to related work; lastly, Section 7 summarises the conclusions drawn from our work and presents possible lines of work.

2 Background

2.1 Annotation based on linked data

Annotating is the process of associating metadata with multimedia assets. Previous research has shown that annotations can benefit from compatibility with linked data technologies (Hausenblas, 2007).

The W3C Open Annotation Community Group has worked towards a common RDF-based specification for annotating digital resources. The group intends to reconcile two previous proposals: the Annotation Ontology (Ciccarese et al., 2011) and the Open Annotation Collaboration (OAC) (Haslhofer et al., 2011). Both proposals incorporate elements from the earlier Annotea model (Kahan et al., 2002). The Open Annotation Ontology (Robert Sanderson and de Sompel, 2013) provides a general description mechanism for sharing annotation between systems based on an RDF model. An annotation is defined by two relationships: *body*, the annotation itself, and *target*, the asset that is annotated. Both body and target can be of any media type. In addition, parts of the body or target can be identified by using Fragment Selectors (oa:FragmentSelector) entities. W3C Fragment URIs (Tennison, 2012) can be used instead, although the use of Fragment Selectors is encouraged. The vocabulary defines fragment selectors for text (oa:Text), text segments plus passages before or after them (oa:TextQuoteSelector), byte streams (oa:DataPositionSelector), areas (oa:AreaSelector), states (oa:State), time moments (oa:TimeState) and request headers (oa:RequestHeaderState). Finally, Open Annotation (OA) ontology defines how annotations are published and transferred between systems. The recommended serialisation format is JSON-LD.

Another research topic has been the standardisation of linguistic annotations in order to improve the interoperability of NLP tools and resources. The main proposals are Linguistic Annotation Framework (LAF) and NIF 2.0. The ISO Specification LAF (Ide and Romary, 2004) and its extension Graph Annotation Format (GrAF) (Ide and Suderman, 2007) define XML serialisation of linguistic annotation as well as RDF mappings. NIF 2.0 (Hellmann et al., 2013) follows a pragmatic approach to linguistic annotations and is focused on interoperability of NLP tools and services. It is directly based on RDF, Linked Data and ontologies, and it allows handling structural interoperability of linguistic annotations as well as semantic interoperability. NIF 2.0 Core ontology provides classes and properties to describe the relationships between substrings, text and documents by assigning URIs to strings. These URIs can then be used as subjects in RDF easily annotated. NIF builds on current best practices for counting strings and creating offsets such as LAF. NIF uses Ontologies for Linguistic Annotation (OLiA) (Chiarcos, 2012) to provide stable identifiers for morpho-syntactical annotation tag sets. In addition to the core ontology, NIF defines Vocabulary modules as an extension mechanism to achieve interoperability between different annotation layers. Some of the defined vocabularies are Marl (Westerski et al., 2011) and Lexicon Model for Ontologies (lemon) (Buitelaar et al., 2011).

As discussed by Hellmann (Hellmann, 2013), the selection of the annotation scheme comes from the domain annotation requirements and the tradeoff among granularity, expressiveness and simplicity. He defines different profiles with this purpose. The profile NIF simple can express *the best estimate* of an NLP tool in a flat data model, with a low number of triples. An intermediate profile called NIF Stanbol allows the inclusion of alternative annotations with different confidence as well as provenance information that can be attached to the additionally created URN for each annotation. This profile is integrated with the semantic content management system Stanbol (Westenhaler, 2014). Finally, the profile NIF OA provides the most expressive model but requires more triples and creates up to four new URNs per annotation, making it more difficult to query.

Finally, we review Fusepool since they propose an annotation model that combines OA and NIF. Fusepool (Westenhaler, 2014) is an R&D project whose purpose is to digest and turn data from different sources into linked data to make data interoperable for reuse. One of the tasks of this project is to define a new Enhancement Structure for the semantic content management system Apache Stanbol (Bachmann-Gmür, 2013). Fusepool researchers' main design considerations with OA is for it to define a very expressive model capable of very complex annotations. This technique comes with the disadvantage of needing a high amount of triples to represent lower level NLP processing, which in turn complicates the queries necessary to retrieve simple data.

2.2 Eurosentiment Model

The work presented here is partly based on an earlier work (Buitelaar et al., 2013) developed within the Eurosentiment project. The Eurosentiment model proposes a linked data approach for sentiment and emotion analysis, and it is based on the following specifications:

- Marl (Westerski et al., 2011) is a vocabulary designed to annotate and describe subjective opinions expressed on the web or in information systems
- Onyx (Sanchez-Rada and Iglesias, 2013) is built on the same principles as Marl to annotate and describe emotions, and provides interoperability with Emotion Markup Language (EmotionML) (Schröder et al., 2011)
- lemon (Buitelaar et al., 2011) defines a lexicon model based on linked data principles which has been extended with Marl and Onyx for sentiment and emotion annotation of lexical entries
- NIF 2.0 (Hellmann et al., 2013) which defines a semantic format and API for improving interoperability among natural language processing services

The way these vocabularies have been integrated is illustrated in the example below, where we are going to analyse the sentiment of an opinion ("Like many Paris hotels, the rooms are too small") posted in TripAdvisor. In the Eurosentiment model, *lemon* is used to define the lexicon for a domain and a language. In our example, we have to generate this lexicon for the hotel domain and the English language[1]. A reduced lexicon for Hotels in English (le:hotel_en) is shown in Listing 1 for illustration purposes. The lexicon is composed of a set of lexical entries (prefix lee). Each lexical entry is semantically disambiguated and provides a reference to the syntactic variant (in the example the canonical form) and the senses. The example shows how the senses have been extended to include sentiment features. In particular, the sense small_1 in the context of room_1 has associated a negative sentiment. That is, "small room" is negative (while small phone could be positive, for example).

[1]The reader interested in how this domain specific lexicon can be generated can consult (Vulcu et al., 2014).

```
lee:sense/small_1 a lemon:Sense;
 lemon:reference "01391351";
 lexinfo:partOfSpeech lexinfo:adjective;
 lemon:context lee:sense/room_1;
 marl:polarityValue "-0.5"^^xsd:double;
 marl:hasPolarity marl:negative.

le:hotel_en a lemon:Lexicon;
 lemon:language "en";
 lemon:topic ed:hotel;
 lemon:entry lee:room, lee:Paris, lee:
    small.

lee:room a lemon:LexicalEntry;
 lemon:canonicalForm [ lemon:writtenRep
     "room"@en ];
 lemon:sense [ lemon:reference wn:synset
     -room-noun-1;
     lemon:reference dbp:Room ];
 lexinfo:partOfSpeech lexinfo:noun.

lee:Paris a lemon:LexicalEntry;
  lemon:canonicalForm [ lemon:writtenRep
      "Paris"@en ];
  lemon:sense [ lemon:reference dbp:
     Paris;
     lemon:reference wn:synset-room-noun
        -1 ];
 lexinfo:partOfSpeech lexinfo:noun.

lee:small a lemon:LexicalEntry;
 lemon:canonicalForm [ lemon:writtenRep
     "small"@en ];
 lemon:sense lee:sense/small_1;
 lexinfo:partOfSpeech lexinfo:adjective.
```

Listing 1: Sentiment analysis expressed with Eurosentiment model.

The Eurosentiment model uses NIF in combination with Marl and Onyx to provide a standardised service interface. In our example, let us assume the opinion has been published at http://tripadvisor.com/myhotel. NIF follows a linked data principled approach so that different tools or services can annotate a text. To this end, texts are converted to RDF literals and an URI is generated so that annotations can be defined for that text in a linked data way. NIF offers different URI Schemes to identify text fragments inside a string, e.g. a scheme based on RFC5147 (Wilde and Duerst, 2008), and a custom scheme based on context. In addition to the format itself, NIF 2.0 defines a REST API for NLP services with standardised parameters. An example of how these ontologies are integrated is illustrated in Listings 2, 3 and 4.

```
<http://tripadvisor.com/myhotel#char
    =0,49>
  rdf:type nif:RDF5147String , nif:
      Context;
  nif:beginIndex "0";
  nif:endIndex "49";
  nif:sourceURL <http://tripadvisor.com/
      myhotel.txt>;
  nif:isString "Like many Paris hotels,
      the rooms are too small";
  marl:hasOpinion <http://tripadvisor.
      com/myhotel/opinion/1>.
```

Listing 2: NIF + Marl output of a service call http://eurosentiment.eu?i=Like many Paris hotels, the rooms are too small

```
<http://tripadvisor.com/myhotel/opinion
    /1>
  rdf:type marl:Opinion;
  marl:describesObject dbp:Hotel;
  marl:describesObjectPart dbp:Room;
  marl:describesFeature  "size";
  marl:polarityValue "-0.5";
  marl:hasPolarity: http://purl.org/marl
      /ns#Negative.
```

Listing 3: Sentiment analysis expressed with Eurosentiment model.

```
<http://eurosentiment.eu/analysis/1>
  rdf:type marl:SentimentAnalysis;
  marl:maxPolarityValue "1";
  marl:minPolarityValue "-1";
  marl:algorithm "dictionary-based";
  prov:used le:hotel_en;
  prov:wasAssociatedWith http://dbpedia.
      org/resource/UPM.
```

Listing 4: Sentiment analysis expressed with Eurosentiment model.

3 Requirements for semantic annotation of sentiment in multimedia resources

The increasing need to deal with human factors, including emotions, on the web has led to the development of the W3C specification EmotionML (Schröder et al., 2011). EmotionML aims for a trade-off between practical applicability and scientific well-foundedness. Given the lack of agreement on a finite set of emotion descriptors, EmotionML follows a plug-in model where emotion vocabularies can be defined depending on the application domain and the aspect of emotions to be focused.

EmotionML (Schröder et al., 2011) uses Media URIs to annotate multimedia assets. Temporal clipping can be specified either as Normal Play Time (npt) (Schulzrinne et al., 1998), as SMPTE timecodes (Society of Motion Picture and Television Engineers, 2009), or as real-world clock time (Schulzrinne et al., 1998).

During the definition of the EmotionML specification, the Emotion Incubator group defined 39 individual use cases (Schröder et al., 2007) that could be grouped into three broad types: manual annotation of materials (e.g. annotation of videos, speech recordings, faces or texts), automatic recognition of emotions from sensors and generation of emotion-related system responses. Based on these uses cases as well as others identified in the literature (Grassi et al., 2011), a number of requirements have been identified for the annotation of multimedia assets based on linked data technologies:

- **Standards compliance**. Emotion annotations should be based on linked data technologies such as RDF or W3C Media Fragment URI. Unfortunately, EmotionML has been defined in XML. Nevertheless, as commented above, the vocabulary Onyx provides a linked data version of EmotionML that can be used instead. Regarding the annotation framework, OA covers the annotation of multimedia assets while NIF only supports the annotation of textual sources.

- **Trace annotation of time-varying signals**. The time curve of properties scales (e.g. arousal or valence) should be preserved. To this end, EmotionML defines two mechanisms. The element *trace* allows the representation of the time evolution of a dynamic scale value based on a periodic sampling of values (i.e. one value every 100ms at 10 Hz). In case of aperiodic sampling, separate emotion annotations should be used. The current version of the ontologies we use does not support trace annotations.

- **Annotations of multimedia fragments**. Fragments of multimedia assets should be enabled. To this end, EmotionML uses Media

URIs to be able to annotate temporal interval or frames. As presented above, NIF provides a compact scheme for textual fragment annotation, but it does not cover multimedia fragments. In contrast, OA supports the annotation of multimedia fragments using a number of triples.

- **Collaborative and multi-modal annotations**. Emotion analysis of multimedia assets may be performed based on different combination of modalities (i.e. full body video, facial video, each with or without speech or textual transcription). Thus, interoperability of emotion annotations is essential. Semantic web technologies provide a solid base for distributed, interoperable and shareable annotations, with proposals such as OA and NIF.

4 Linked Data Annotation for Multimedia Sentiment Analysis

One of the main goals of NIF is interoperability between NLP tools. For this, it uses a convention to assign URIs to parts of a text. Since URIs are unique, different tools can analyse the same text independently, and one may use the URIs later to combine the information from both.

These URIs are constructed with a combination of the URI of the source of the string (its context), and a unique identifier for that string within that particular context. A way to assign that identifier is called a URI scheme. Strings belong to different classes, according to the scheme used to generate its URI. The currently available schemes are: ContextHashBasedString, OffsetBasedString, RFC5147String and ArbitraryString. The usual scheme is *RFC5147String*.

For instance, for a context `http://example.com`, its content may be "This is a test", and the *RFC5147String* `http://example.com#char=5,7` would refer to the "is" part within the context.

However, to annotate multimedia sources indexing by characters is obviously not possible. We need a different way to uniquely refer to a fragment.

Among the different possible approaches to identify media elements, we propose to follow the same path as the Ontology for Media Resources (Lee et al., 2012) and use the Media Fragments URI W3C recommendation (Troncy et al., 2012). The recommendation specifies how to refer to a specific fragment or subpart of a media resource. URIs follow this scheme:

<scheme>:<part>[?<q>][#<frag.>]

Where <scheme> is the specific scheme or protocol (e.g. http), part is the hierarchical part (e.g. example.com), q is the query (e.g. user=Nobody), and frag is the piece we are interested in: the multimedia fragment (e.g. t=10).

Since the Media Fragments URI schema is very similar to those already used in NIF and follows the same philosophy, we have extended NIF to include it. The result is Figure 1.

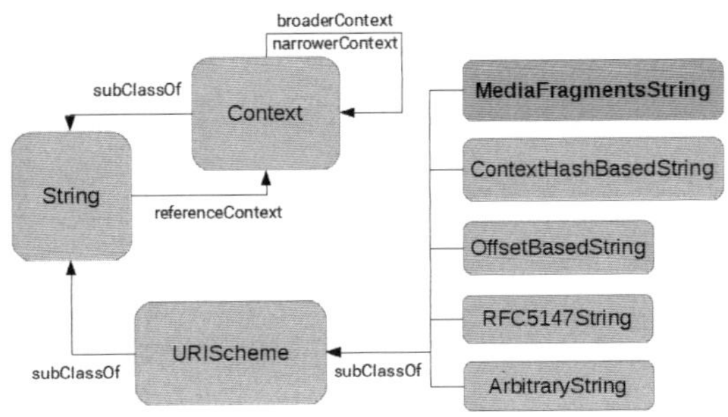

Figure 1: By extending the URI Schemes of NIF, we make it possible to use multimedia sources in NIF, and refer to their origin using the Media Fragments recommendation.

Using this URI Scheme and the NIF notation for sentiment analysis, the results from a service that analyses both the captions from a YouTube video and the video comments would look like the document in Listing 5. In this way, we fulfill the requirements previously identified in Sect. 3. This example is, in fact, the aggregation of three different kinds of analysis: textual sentiment analysis on comments (`CommentAnalysis`) and captions (`CaptionAnalysis`), and sentiment analysis based on facial expressions (`SmileAnalysis`). Each analysis would individually return a document similar to that of the example, with only the fields corresponding to that particular analysis.

The results can be summarised as follows: a youtube video (`http://youtu.be/W07PoKUD-Yk`) is tagged as positive overall based on facial expressions (`OpinionS01`); the section of the video from second 108 to second 110 (`http://youtu.be/W07PoKUD-Yk#t=108,110`) reflects negative sentiment judging by the captions (`OpinionT01`);

lastly, the video has a comment (http://www.youtube.com/comment?lc=<CommentID>) that reflects a positive opinion (OpinionC01).

The JSON-LD context in Listing 6 provides extra information the semantics of the document, and has been added for completeness.

```
{
"analysis": [{
 "@id": "SmileAnalysis",
 "@type": "marl:SentimentAnalysis",
 "marl:algorithm": "AverageSmiles"
 }, {
 "@id": "CaptionAnalysis",
 "@type": "marl:SentimentAnalysis",
 "marl:algorithm": "NaiveBayes"
 }, {
 "@id": "CommentAnalysis",
 "@type": "marl:SentimentAnalysis",
 "marl:algorithm": "NaiveBayes"
 }],
"entries": [{
 "@id": "http://youtu.be/W07PoKUD-Yk",
 "@type": [
  "nifmedia:MediaFragmentsString",
  "nif:Context"],
 "nif:isString": "<FULL Transcript>",
 "opinions": [{
  "@id": "_:OpinionS01",
  "marl:hasPolarity": "marl:Positive",
  "marl:polarityValue": 0.5,
  "prov:generatedBy": "SmileAnalysis"
  }],
 "sioc:hasReply": "http://
    ↪ www.youtube.com/comment?lc=<
    ↪ CommentID>",
 "strings": [{
  "@id": "http://youtu.be/W07PoKUD-Yk#t=
     ↪ 108,110",
  "@type": "nifmedia:
     ↪ MediaFragmentsString",
  "nif:anchorOf": "Family budgets under
     ↪ pressure",
  "opinions": [{
   "@id": "_:OpinionT01",
   "marl:hasPolarity": "marl:Negative",
   "marl:polarityValue": -0.3058,
   "prov:generatedBy": "CaptionAnalysis"
   }]
 }]
 }, {
 "@id": "http://www.youtube.com/comment?
    ↪ lc=<CommentID>",
 "@type": [
  "nif:Context", "nif:RFC5147String" ],
 "nif:isString": "He is well spoken",
 "opinions": [{
  "@id": "OpinionC01",
  "marl:hasPolarity": "marl:Positive",
  "marl:polarityValue": 1,
  "prov:generatedBy": "CommentAnalysis"
  }]
 }]
}
```

Listing 5: Service results are annotated on the fragment level with sentiment and any other property in NIF such as POS tags or entities.

```
{
 "marl": "http://www.gsi.dit.upm.es/
    ↪ ontologies/marl/ns#",
 "nif": "http://persistence.uni-
    ↪ leipzig.org/nlp2rdf/ontologies/
    ↪ nif-core#",
 "onyx": "http://www.gsi.dit.upm.es/
    ↪ ontologies/onyx/ns#",
 "nifmedia": "http://www.gsi.dit.upm.es/
    ↪ ontologies/nif/ns#",
 "analysis": {
    "@id": "prov:wasInformedBy"
 },
 "opinions": {
   "@container": "@list",
   "@id": "marl:hasOpinion",
   "@type": "marl:Opinion"
 },
 "entries": {
    "@id": "prov:generated"
 },
 "strings": {
    "@reverse": "nif:hasContext"
 }
}
```

Listing 6: JSON-LD context for the results necessary to give semantic meaning to the JSON in Listing 5.

5 Application

5.1 VESA: Online HTML5 Video Annotator

The first application to use NIF annotation for sentiment analysis of Multimedia sources is VESA, the Video Emotion and Sentiment Analysis tool. VESA is both a tool to run sentiment analysis of online videos, and a visualisation tool which shows the evolution of sentiment information and the transcript as the video is playing, using HTML5 widgets. The visualisation tool can run the analysis in real time (live analysis) or use previously stored results.

The live analysis generates transcriptions using the built-in Web Speech API in Google Chrome[2] while the video plays in the background. To improve the performance and accuracy of the transcription process, the audio is chunked in sentences (delimited by a silence). Then, each chunk is sent to a sentiment analysis service. As of this writing, users can choose sentiment analysis in Spanish or English, in a general or a financial domain, using different dictionaries.

The evolution of sentiment within the video is shown as a graph below the video in Figure 2. The

[2]https://www.google.com/intl/en/chrome/demos/speech.html

full transcript of the video allows users to check the accuracy of the transcription service.

The results from the service can be stored in a database, and can be later replayed. We also developed a Widget version of the annotator that can be embedded in other websites, and integrated in widget frameworks like Sefarad[3].

The project is completely open source and can be downloaded from its Github repository[4].

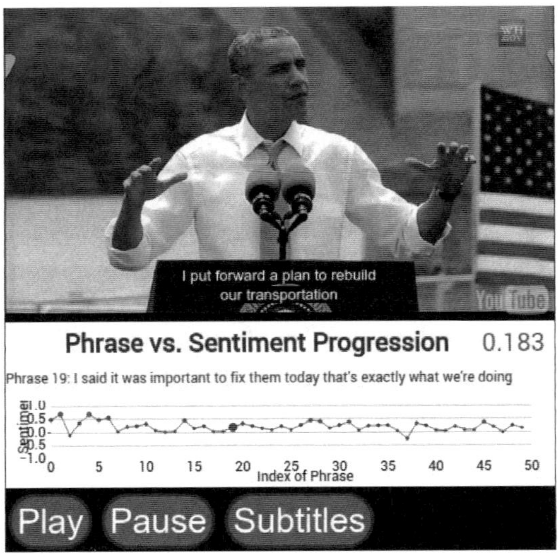

Figure 2: The graph shows the detected sentiment in the video over time, while the video keeps playing.

5.2 Semantic multimodal queries

This section demonstrates how it would be possible to integrate sentiment analysis of different modes using SPARQL. In particular, it covers two scenarios: fusion of results from different modes, and detection of complex patterns using information from several modes.

As discussed in Section 6, SPARQL has some limitations when it comes to querying media fragments. There are extensions to SPARQL that overcome those limitations. However, for the sake of clarity, this section will avoid those extensions. Instead, the examples assume that the original media is chunked equally for every mode. Every chunk represents a media fragment, which may contain an opinion.

[3] http://github.com/gsi-upm/Sefarad

[4] https://github.com/gsi-upm/video-sentiment-analysis

When different modes yield different sentiments or emotions, it is usually desirable to integrate all the results into a single one. The query in Listing 7 shows how to retrieve all the opinions for each chunk. These results can be fed to a fusion algorithm.

```
SELECT ?frag ?algo ?opinion ?pol WHERE {
  ?frag a nifmedia:MediaFragmentsString;
        marl:hasOpinion ?opinion.
  ?opinion marl:hasPolarity ?pol.
  ?algo prov:generated ?opinion.
}
```

Listing 7: Gathering all the opinions detected in a video.

Another possibility is that the discrepancies between different modes reveal useful information. For instance, using a cheerful tone of voice for a negative text may indicate sarcasm or untruthfulness. Listing 8 shows an example of how to detect such discrepancies. Note that it uses both opinions and emotions at the same time.

```
SELECT ?frag WHERE {
  ?frag a nifmedia:MediaFragmentsString;
        marl:hasOpinion ?opinion;
        onyx:hasEmotion ?emo.
  ?opinion prov:wasGeneratedBy
              _:TextAnalysis;
           marl:hasPolarity marl:
              Negative.
  ?emo prov:wasGeneratedBy
              _:AudioAnalysis;
       onyx:hasEmotionCategory wna:
          Cheerfulness.
}
```

Listing 8: Detecting negative text narrated with a cheerful tone of voice.

6 Related work

Semedi research group proposes the use of semantic web technologies for video fragment annotation (Morbidoni et al., 2011) and affective states based on the HEO (Grassi et al., 2011) ontology. They propose the use of standards, such as XPointer (Paul Grosso and Walsh, 2003) and Media Fragment URI (Troncy et al., 2012) for defining URIs for text and multimedia, respectively, as well as the Open Annotation Ontology (Robert Sanderson and de Sompel, 2013) for expressing the annotations. Their approach is similar to the one we have proposed, based on web standards and linked data to express emotion annotations. Our proposal has been aligned with the latest available specifications, which have been extended as presented in this article.

On the other hand, a better integration between multimedia and the linked data toolbox would be necessary. Working with multimedia fragments in plain SPARQL is not an easy task. More specifically, it is the relationship between fragments that complicates it, e.g. finding overlaps or contiguous segments. An extension to SPARQL by Kurz et al. (Kurz et al., 2014), SPARQL-MM, introduces convenient methods that allow these operations in a concise way.

7 Conclusions and future work

We have introduced the conceptual tools to describe sentiment and emotion analysis results in a semantic format, not only from textual sources but also multimedia.

Despite being primarily oriented towards analysis of texts extracted from multimedia sources, this approach can be used to apply other kinds of analysis, in a way similar to how NIF integrates results from different tools. However, more effort needs to be put into exploring different use cases and how they can be integrated in our extension of NIF for sentiment analysis in multimedia. This work will be done in the project MixedEmotions, where several use cases (Brand Monitoring, Social TV or Call Center Management) have been identified and involve multimedia analysis.

In addition, this discussion can be carried out in the *Linked Data Models for Emotion and Sentiment Analysis* W3C Community Group [5], where professionals and academics of the Semantic and sentiment analysis worlds meet and discuss the application of an interdisciplinary approach.

Regarding the video annotator, although the current version is fully functional, it could be improved in several ways. The main limitation is that its live analysis relies on the Web Speech API, and needs user interaction to set specific audio settings. We are studying other fully client-side approaches.

Acknowledgements

This research has been partially funded and by the EC through the H2020 project MixedEmotions (Grant Agreement no: 141111) and by the Spanish Ministry of Industry, Tourism and Trade through the project Calista (TEC2012-32457).

The authors also want to thank Berto Yáñez for his support and inspiring demo "Popcorn.js Sentiment Tracker".

[5] `http://www.w3.org/community/sentiment/`

References

Reto Bachmann-Gmür. 2013. *Instant Apache Stanbol*. Packt Publisher.

Paul Buitelaar, Philipp Cimiano, John McCrae, Elena Montiel-Ponsoda, and Thierry Declerck. 2011. Ontology lexicalisation: The lemon perspective. In *Workshop at 9th International Conference on Terminology and Artificial Intelligence (TIA 2011)*, pages 33–36.

Paul Buitelaar, Mihael Arcan, Carlos A Iglesias, J Fernando Sánchez-Rada, and Carlo Strapparava. 2013. Linguistic linked data for sentiment analysis. In *2nd Workshop on Linked Data in Linguistics (LDL-2013): Representing and linking lexicons, terminologies and other language data*, Pisa, Italy.

Christian Chiarcos. 2012. Ontologies of linguistic annotation: Survey and perspectives. In *LREC*, pages 303–310.

Paolo Ciccarese, Marco Ocana, Leyla Jael Garcia-Castro, Sudeshna Das, and Tim Clark. 2011. An open annotation ontology for science on web 3.0. *J. Biomedical Semantics*, 2(S-2):S4.

Marco Grassi, Christian Morbidoni, and Francesco Piazza. 2011. Towards semantic multimodal video annotation. In *Toward Autonomous, Adaptive, and Context-Aware Multimodal Interfaces. Theoretical and Practical Issues*, volume 6456 of *Lecture Notes in Computer Science*, pages 305–316. Springer Berlin Heidelberg.

Bernhard Haslhofer, Rainer Simon, Robert Sanderson, and Herbert Van de Sompel. 2011. The open annotation collaboration (oac) model. In *Multimedia on the Web (MMWeb), 2011 Workshop on*, pages 5–9. IEEE.

Michael Hausenblas. 2007. Multimedia vocabularies on the semantic web. Technical report, World Wide Web (W3C).

Sebastian Hellmann, Jens Lehmann, Sören Auer, and Martin Brümmer. 2013. Integrating nlp using linked data. In *The Semantic Web–ISWC 2013*, pages 98–113. Springer.

Sebastian Hellmann. 2013. *Integrating Natural Language Processing (NLP) and Language Resources using Linked Data*. Ph.D. thesis, Universität Leipzig.

Nancy Ide and Laurent Romary. 2004. International standard for a linguistic annotation framework. *Natural language engineering*, 10(3-4):211–225.

Nancy Ide and Keith Suderman. 2007. Graf: A graph-based format for linguistic annotations. In *Proceedings of the Linguistic Annotation Workshop*, LAW '07, pages 1–8, Stroudsburg, PA, USA. Association for Computational Linguistics.

J. Kahan, M.-R. Koivunen, E. Prud'Hommeaux, and R.R. Swick. 2002. Annotea: an open {RDF} infrastructure for shared web annotations. *Computer Networks*, 39(5):589 – 608.

Thomas Kurz, Sebastian Schaffert, Kai Schlegel, Florian Stegmaier, and Harald Kosch. 2014. Sparql-mm-extending sparql to media fragments. In *The Semantic Web: ESWC 2014 Satellite Events*, pages 236–240. Springer.

WonSuk Lee, Werner Bailer, Tobias Bürger, Pierre-Antoine Champin, Jean-Pierre Evain, Véronique Malaisé, Thierry Michel, Felix Sasaki, Joakim Söderberg, Florian Stegmaier, and John Strassner. 2012. Ontology for Media Resources 1.0. Technical report, World Wide Web Consortium (W3C), February. Available at http://www.w3.org/TR/mediaont-10/.

C. Morbidoni, M. Grassi, M. Nucci, S. Fonda, and G. Ledda. 2011. Introducing semlib project: semantic web tools for digital libraries. *International Workshop on Semantic Digital Archives-Sustainable Long-term Curation Perspectives of Cultural Heritage Held as Part of the 15th International Conference on Theory and Practice of Digital Libraries (TPDL), Berlin.*

Jonathan Marsh Paul Grosso, Eve Mater and Normal Walsh. 2003. W3C XPointer Framework. Technical report, World Wide Web Consortium (W3C), March. Available at http://www.w3.org/TR/xptr-framework/.

Pablo Ciccarese Robert Sanderson and Herbert Van de Sompel. 2013. W3C Open Annotation Data Model. Technical report, World Wide Web Consortium (W3C), February. Available at http://www.openannotation.org/spec/core/.

J Fernando Sanchez-Rada and Carlos Angel Iglesias. 2013. Onyx: Describing emotions on the web of data. In *ESSEM@ AI* IA*, pages 71–82. Citeseer.

Marc Schröder, Enrico Zovato, Hannes Pirker, Christian Peter, and Felix Burkhardt. 2007. W3C Emotion Incubator Group Report 10 July 2007. Technical report, W3C, July. Available at http://www.w3.org/2005/Incubator/emotion/XGR-emotion/.

Marc Schröder, Paolo Baggia, Felix Burkhardt, Catherine Pelachaud, Christian Peter, and Enrico Zovato. 2011. Emotionml – an upcoming standard for representing emotions and related states. In Sidney D'Mello, Arthur Graesser, Björn Schuller, and Jean-Claude Martin, editors, *Affective Computing and Intelligent Interaction*, volume 6974 of *Lecture Notes in Computer Science*, pages 316–325. Springer Berlin Heidelberg.

H. Schulzrinne, A. Rao, and R. Lanphier. 1998. Real Time Streaming Protocol (RTP). Technical Report RFC2326, IETF. Available at http://www.ietf.org/rfc/rfc2326.txt.

Society of Motion Picture and Television Engineers. 2009. SMPTE - RP 136. time and control codes for 24, 25 or 30 frame-per-second motion-picture systems - stabilized 2009. Technical report, SMPTE.

Jeni Tennison. 2012. Best practices for fragment identifiers and media type definitions. Technical report, World Wide Web (W3C).

Raphaël Troncy, Erik Mannens, Silvia Pfeiffer, and Davy Van Deursen. 2012. W3C Recommendation Media Fragments URI 1.0. Technical report, World Wide Web Consortium (W3C), September. Available at http://www.w3.org/TR/2012/REC-media-frags-20120925/.

Gabriela Vulcu, Paul Buitelaar, Sapna Negi, Bianca Pereira, Mihael Arcan, Barry Coughlan, J. Fernando Sánchez-Rada, and Carlos A. Iglesias. 2014. Generating Linked-Data based Domain-Specific Sentiment Lexicons from Legacy Language and Semantic Resources. In *th International Workshop on Emotion, Social Signals, Sentiment & Linked Open Data, co-located with LREC 2014*, Reykjavik, Iceland, May. LREC2014.

Rupert Westenhaler. 2014. Open Annotation and NIF 2.0 based Annotation Model for Apache Stanbol. In *Proceedings of ISWC 2014*.

Adam Westerski, Carlos A. Iglesias, and Fernando Tapia. 2011. Linked opinions: Describing sentiments on the structured web of data.

E. Wilde and M. Duerst. 2008. URI Fragment Identifiers for the text/plain Media Type. Technical Report RDF5147, Internet Engineering Task Force (IETF), April. Available at https://tools.ietf.org/html/rfc5147.

Seeing is Correcting: curating lexical resources using social interfaces

Livy Real
IBM Research
livyreal@gmail.com

Fabricio Chalub
IBM Research
fcbrbr@gmail.com

Valeria de Paiva
Nuance Communications
valeria.depaiva@gmail.com

Claudia Freitas
PUC-RJ
maclaudia.freitas@gmail.com

Alexandre Rademaker
IBM Research and FGV/EMAp
alexrad@br.ibm.com

Abstract

This note describes OpenWordnet-PT, an automatically created, manually curated wordnet for Portuguese and introduces the newly developed web interface we are using to speed up its manual curation. OpenWordNet-PT is part of a collection of wordnets for various languages, jointly described and distributed through the Open Multi-Lingual WordNet and the Global WordNet Association. OpenWordnet-PT has been primarily distributed, from the beginning, as RDF files along with its model description in OWL, and it is freely available for download. We contend the creation of such large, distributed and linkable lexical resources is on the cusp of revolutionizing multilingual language processing to the next truly semantic level. But to get there, there is a need for user interfaces that allow ordinary users and (not only computational) linguists to help in the checking and cleaning up of the quality of the resource. We present our suggestion of one such web interface and describe its features supporting the collaborative curation of the data. This showcases the use and importance of its linked data features, to keep track of information provenance during the whole life-cycle of the RDF resource.

1 Introduction

Lexical knowledge bases are organized repositories of information about words. These resources typically include information about the possible meanings of words, relations between these meanings, definitions and phrases that exemplify their use and maybe some numeric grades of confidence in the information provided. The Princeton wordnet model (Fellbaum, 1998), with English as its target language, is probably the most popular model of a lexical knowledge base. Our main goal is to provide good quality lexical resources for Portuguese, making use, as much as possible, of the effort already spent creating similar resources for English. Thus we are working towards a Portuguese wordnet, based on the Princeton model (de Paiva et al., 2012).

Linguistic resources are very easy to start working on, very hard to improve and extremely difficult to maintain, as the last two tasks do not get the recognition that the first one gets. Given this intrinsic barrier, many well-funded projects, with institutional or commercial backing cannot keep their momentum. Thus it is rather pleasing to see that a project like ours, without any kind of official infra-structure, has been able to continue development and improvement so far, re-inventing its tools and methods, to the extent that it has been chosen by Google Translate to be used as their source of lexical information for Portuguese[1].

This paper reports on a new web interface[2] for consulting, checking and collaborating on the improvement of OpenWordnet-PT. This is the automatically created, but manually verified wordnet for Portuguese, fully compatible and connected to Princeton's paradigmatic WordNet, that we are working on. It has been surprising how a simple interface can make content so much more perspicuous. Thus our title: if seeing is believing, new ways of seeing the data and of slicing it, according to our requirements, are necessary for curating, correcting and improving this data.

Correcting and improving linguistic data is a hard task, as the guidelines for what to aim for are not set in stone nor really known in advance. While the WordNet model has been paradigmatic in modern computational lexicography, this model is not without its failings and shortcomings, as far as specific tasks are concerned. Also it is easy and somewhat satisfying to provide copious quantitative descriptions of numbers of synsets, for different parts-of-speech, of triples associated to these synsets and of intersections with different subsets

[1] http://translate.google.com/about/intl/en_ALL/license.html

[2] http://wnpt.brlcloud.com/wn/

Proceedings of the 4th Workshop on Linked Data in Linguistics (LDL-2015), pages 20–29,
Beijing, China, July 31, 2015.

of Wordnet, etc. However, the whole community dedicated to creating wordnets in other languages, the Global WordNet Association[3], has not come up with criteria for semantic evaluation of these resources nor has it produced, so far, ways of comparing their relative quality or accuracy. Thus qualitative assessment of a new wordnet seems, presently, a matter of judgement and art, more than a commonly agreed practice. Believing that this qualitative assessment is important, and so far rather elusive, we propose in this note that having many eyes over the resource, with the ability to shape it in the directions wanted, is a main advantage. This notion of volunteer curated content, as first and foremost exemplified by Wikipedia, needs adaptation to work for lexical resources. This paper describes one such adaptation.

2 OpenWordnet-PT

The OpenWordnet-PT (Rademaker et al., 2014), abbreviated as OpenWN-PT, is a wordnet originally developed as a syntactic projection of the Universal WordNet (UWN) of de Melo and Weikum (de Melo and Weikum, 2009). Its long term goal is to serve as the main lexicon for a system of natural language processing focused on logical reasoning, based on representation of knowledge, using an ontology, such as SUMO (Pease and Fellbaum, 2010).

OpenWN-PT was built using machine learning techniques to create relations between graphs representing lexical information coming from versions (in multiple languages) of Wikipedia entries and open electronic dictionaries. For details, one can consult (de Melo and Weikum, 2009). Then a projection targeting only the synsets in Portuguese was produced. Despite starting out as a projection only, at the level of the lemmas in Portuguese and their relationships, the OpenWN-PT has been constantly improved through *linguistically motivated* additions and removals, either manually or by making use of large corpora.

The philosophy of OpenWN-PT is to maintain a close connection with Princeton's wordnet since this minimizes the impact of lexicographical decisions on the separation or grouping of senses in a given synset. Such disambiguation decisions are inherently arbitrary (Kilgarriff, 1997), thus the multilingual alignment gives us a pragmatic and practical solution. The solution of following the work in Princeton is practical, as WordNet remains the most used lexical resource in the world. It is also pragmatic, since those decisions will be more useful, if they are similar to what other wordnets say. Of course this does not mean that all decisions will be sorted out for us. As part of our processing is automated and error-prone, we strive to remove the biggest mistakes created by automation, using linguistic skills and tools. In this endeavour we are much helped by the linked data philosophy and implementation, as keeping the alignment between synsets is facilitated by looking at the synsets in several different languages in parallel. For this we make use of the Open Multilingual WordNet's interface (Bond and Foster, 2013).

This lexical enrichment process of OpenWN-PT employs three language strategies: (i) translation; (ii) corpus extraction; (iii) dictionaries. Regarding translations, glossaries and lists produced for other languages, such as English, French and Spanish are used, automatically translated and manually revised. The addition of corpora data contributes words or phrases in common use which may be specific to the Portuguese language (e.g. the verb *frevar*, which means to dance *frevo*, a typical Brazilian dance) or which do not appear via the automatic construction, for some reason. (One can conjecture that perhaps the word is too rare for the automatic methods to pick it up: an example would be the adjective *hidrogenada*, which is in use in every supermarket of Brasil. The verb *hydrogenate* is in the English wordnet, the verb exists exactly as expected in Portuguese *hidrogenar*, but the automatic methods did not find it nor the derived adjective.) The first corpora experiment in OpenWN-PT was the integration of the nominalizations lexicon, the NomLex-PT (Freitas et al., 2014). Use of a corpus, while helpful for specific conceptualizations in the language, brings additional challenges for mapping alignment, since it is expected that there will be expressions for which there is no synset in the English wordnet. Dictionaries were used both for the original creation of Portuguese synsets but also indirectly through the linguists' use of PAPEL (Gonçalo Oliveira et al., 2008) to construct extra pairs of words of the form (verb, nominalization).

3 Current status

The OpenWN-PT currently has 43,925 synsets, of which 32,696 correspond to nouns, 4,675 to verbs,

[3]`http://globalwordnet.org/`

5,575 to adjectives and 979 to adverbs. While it is not as comprehensive as Princeton's, the Finnish, or the Thai wordnets, it is still more than twice the size of the Russian wordnet, bigger than the Spanish and just a little smaller than the French wordnet. But as discussed in the introduction, the quality of these resources is much harder to compare.

Besides downloading it, the data on Portuguese can be retrieved via a SPARQL endpoint [4]. The multilingual base can be consulted and compared with other wordnets using the Open Multilingual Wordnet (OMWN) interface [5] and changing preferences to the desired languages, assuming the lexical item is found [6].

The ability of comparing senses in several languages was already useful when judging meanings in Portuguese. However, before the new interface was implemented, we did not the ability to compare a word with the collection of other words with the same meaning, or with different shades of meaning, appearing both in English and Portuguese. This all changed, since we started developing a new search and editing interface in September 2014.

4 Challenges of lexical enrichment

We set ourselves the task of building a wordnet for Portuguese, based on the Princeton wordnet model. This is not the same as building the Princeton wordnet in Portuguese. We do not propose to simply translate the original wordnet, but mean to create a wordnet for Portuguese based on Princeton's architecture and, as much as possible, linked to it at the level of the synsets.

The task of building a wordnet in Portuguese imposes many challenges and choices. Even the simple translation of a lexical resource, such as NomLex (Catherine Macleod, 1998) for comparison and further extension of our wordnet, requires different techniques and theoretical decisions. One example might help: the synsets automatically provided by OpenWN-PT tend to have relatively high register words, especially ones with Latin or Greek roots and present in several European languages. Thus we do not get many colloquialisms or everyday words from the translation dictionaries that are the sources for our wordnet. Worse, even when there is more than one possible translation of an English word, there is no way to make sure that the automatic process gets the most used variant in Portuguese. Thus we have to compensate and complete our synsets and many choices are necessary. These lexical choices have direct consequences on the type and quality of the resource been built.

This section discusses some of the problems and issues we have when trying to deal with the mistakes we perceive in OpenWordnet-PT and principally how to deal with senses in wordnet that do not have a clearly corresponding sense in Portuguese.

Our most important decisions so far were related to (i) which variants of Portuguese to treat, (ii) how to deal with mistakes, ungrammaticalities and other problems in our entries, (iii) how to deal with senses in wordnet that apparently do not have a straightforward corresponding sense in Portuguese and (iv) how to add senses in Portuguese that do not seem to exist in English (or at least in the Princeton's version).

We have decided that OpenWN-PT should, in principle, include all variants of Portuguese. First because European Portuguese and Brazilian Portuguese are not that different, then because there is a single Wikipedia/Wiktionary in Portuguese but mostly because it is more complicated to decide which words are used where, than to be inclusive and have all variants. Thus senses that can be expressed through words that have different spellings on different Portuguese dialects (e.g. *gênio, génio*) should include all these variants.

First, to clean up our knowledge base, we still have to remove some Spanish, Galician or Catalan words that are easily misjudged as Portuguese by the automatic processing. We also have to make sure that the part of speech (POS) classification is preserved: many times the popularity driven automatic process prefers the noun meaning of a verb that can be both, or conversely. For example in the noun synset `06688274-n` the automatic processing chose the verb *creditar* 'to credit' instead of the related noun *crédito* 'credit'. We also have several problems with the lemmatization and capitalization of entries, as criteria for the use of capitals are different in English and Portuguese and our entries were not lemmatized beforehand. We follow

[4] `http://logics.emap.fgv.br:10035/repositories/wn30`

[5] `http://compling.hss.ntu.edu.sg/omw`

[6] Since we do not have control over the update processes of OMWN the reader should be aware that OMWN might be not up-to-date with the current OpenWN-PT version.

the Portuguese dictionary traditions and mostly only list the masculine singular form of nouns and adjectives.

Much more complicated than the cleaning up task is the issue (iii) of Princeton wordnet's concepts that do not have a exact, single word correspondent in Portuguese. Several, related problems can be seen here. The original WordNet has many multi-word expressions as part of its synsets. The proverbial *kick the bucket* (and one of its corresponding idiomatic Portuguese expressions *bater as botas* – literally *click the boots*) comes to mind. Thus we do not have a problem with the idea of using expressions, but we do have a problem in deciding which kinds of expressions should be considered in Portuguese. For one example, we do not have a verb corresponding to *to jog* in Portuguese. People use *correr* which means *to run*, but this is not quite right. For one, running is faster than jogging, so jogging is a slow running, and then jogging is for fun or exercise, as WordNet tells us. The Anglicism *fazer jogging* is also very used in Brazil and forces us to think about how 'truly Portuguese' should our entries be.

Another kind of example of English synsets that have no exact Portuguese words at the moment, but it is easier to deal with, is a synset like `08139795-n`, which corresponds to the United States Department of the Treasury. This is a named organization. Should it be in a Portuguese wordnet? Which instances of entities should a wordnet carry? All the names of countries and cities and regions of the world? There are specialized resources like GeoNames that might be much better equipped for that. Which famous people and companies and organizations should a dictionary or a thesaurus have? Again encyclopedic resources like Wikipedia, DBpedia or Wikidata seem much more appropriate. This is what we call amongst ourselves the *A-Box problem*, in a reference to the way Description Logics classify statements. Having translations for all these A-box instances causes us no problem, but not having them is not a big issue either, if we have other sources of information to rely on.

For a third, perhaps harder example, consider the synset `13390244-n`, which uses a specific word (a 'quarter') for the concept of "a United States or Canadian coin worth one fourth of a dollar". We have no reason to have this concept in a Portuguese wordnet and we have no word for it in Portuguese. But we can use a commom expression, such as *moeda de 25 centavos [de dolar]*, for it. Although '25 cents coin', strictly speaking, might not be the same concept as 'quarter'. This will depend on which notion of equality of concepts you are willing to use, a much harder discussion.

For now, for the general problem of what to do with synsets that have no exact corresponding word or synset, we have no clear theoretical decisions or guidelines in place, yet. These problems are still being decided, via a lazy strategy of cleaning up what is clearly wrong first, and collecting subsidies for the more intricate lexicographic decisions later on. Some of these discussions and decisions were described in (de Paiva et al., 2014).

We are not yet working on the Portuguese senses that do not seem to have a corresponding synset in Princeton's wordnet (issue (iv) above). An example might be *jogo de cintura*, which means a property of someone who can easily adapt his/her aims and feelings to a certain situation (the literal meaning is more like "[have] hip moves"). We will add in these new synsets, once we finish the first version of a cleaned up OpenWN-PT that we are completing at the moment. For the time being, we are simply collecting interesting examples of Portuguese words that do not seem to have a direct translation, such as *avacalhar, encafifar*.

But apart from phenomena that have to be dealt with in a uniform way, we have also one-off disambiguation problems, like the verb *to date=datar*, that in Portuguese is only used to put a date (on to a document, a monument or a rock), when in English it also means *to go out with*. Thus the automatic processing ended up with a synset meaning both "finding the age of" and "going out with", `00619183-v`, which is a bad mistake. To see and check this kind of situation, it was decided that the interface would allow linguists to accept or remove a word, a gloss and examples of the use of the synset.

5 The New Interface

The need for an online and searchable version of OpenWN-PT arises for two reasons: (i) to have an accessible tool for end users, (ii) to improve our strategy to correct and improve the resource. As far as being accessible to end users the open source interface, available from GitHub [7] seems

[7] `https://github.com/fcbr/cl-wnbrowser`

a success: after a couple of months online, we have gathered over 4000 suggestions from the web interface, incorporated over 125000 suggestions from automatic processes that are being evaluated, and over 7000 votes have been cast. As for the social/discussion aspect, over 2600 comments have been made on the system and we have registered some sort of conflict in over a hundred suggestions (where we have votes agreeing and disagreeing over the same suggestion). All this being done by a team of five people, where usually two and three are mostly active. More usage statistics are being collected, but it seems clear that it is useful. Considering (ii), our main purpose with the new interface is to edit the entries of OpenWN-PT as they exist. The first design decision was that before adding new synsets corresponding to the Portuguese reality, we should clean up the network from its most egregious mistakes, caused by the automatic processing of the entries.

Figure 1 shows how a synset appears in the new interface. Note the *voting mechanism*, vaguely inspired by Reddit. Trusted users vote for their desired modifications. Here the expression *sair com* has been voted to be removed, three times. There are also links to the same synset in SUMO and OMW.

We encourage the collaborative revision of OpenWN-PT and have been working on guidelines to foster consistency of suggestions. These describe the desired format of examples, glosses and variations of the words in synsets. The preliminary and evolving guidelines for annotators are now available online[8] and we also started documenting the features of the system for end users[9].

But the new interface was much more useful than simply offering the possibility of local rewrites, as it has allowed us to make faceted search for different classes of synsets and of words, both in English and in Portuguese.

Figure 2 shows the synsets that have no words in Portuguese (via facets on the number of words in English and Portuguese), which allows us to target these synsets and to decide whether they are simply missing a not very popular word (e.g. `00117230-v` is missing the not terribly interesting verb *opalizar*, an exact correspondent to *opalize*) or they correspond to a sense that does not work exactly the same way in English and Portuguese. For example, back to the verb *to date* as in *romantically going out with someone*, English seems to leave underspecified whether it is a habitual event or a single one, while in Portuguese we use different verbs, *namorar* or *sair*, but if we want to not commit ourselves to either kind of engagement, we use the verbal expression *sair com*.

Regarding the technologies adopted for development, the interface runs on the IBM BlueMix(blu,) cloud platform implemented in three layers. A Cloudant(clo,) database service for data storage is queried and updated via an API written in NodeJS(nod,). The user interface is coded in Common Lisp using a collection of packages for web development, such as `hunchentoot`, `closure-template`, and `yason`. We have plans to increase the use of Javascript libraries to make the interface more usable, responsive, and mobile-friendly.

Our principal goal in developing the web interface is to provide an application that supports the achievement of consensus in the manual revisions. For this, we follow certain aspects commonly used in social networking websites, such as votes and comments. Contributors can submit suggestions and vote on already submitted suggestions. While anyone can submit any suggestion, in this initial phase only selected users can vote. We currently specify that we need at least three positive votes to accept a suggestion, but two negative votes are enough to reject it. A batch process counts the votes every night and accepts/rejects the suggestions. Finally, another batch process commits the accepted suggestions in the data, removing or adding new information. This modular architecture provides good performance and maintainability. We never delete suggestions, even the rejected ones. This way we keep track of the provenance of all changes in the data.

We encourage patterns of communication between users frequently associated with social networks such as Twitter and Reddit where users can mention other users in comments (thus asking for attention on that particular topic). Comments may also contain 'hash tags' that are used, for instance, to tag particular synsets for later consideration by other users.

6 Linked Data Rationale

As it is well-known linked data, as proposed by (Berners-Lee, 2011), has four main principles for

[8] `https://goo.gl/tIROu0`
[9] `https://goo.gl/yzXVR9`

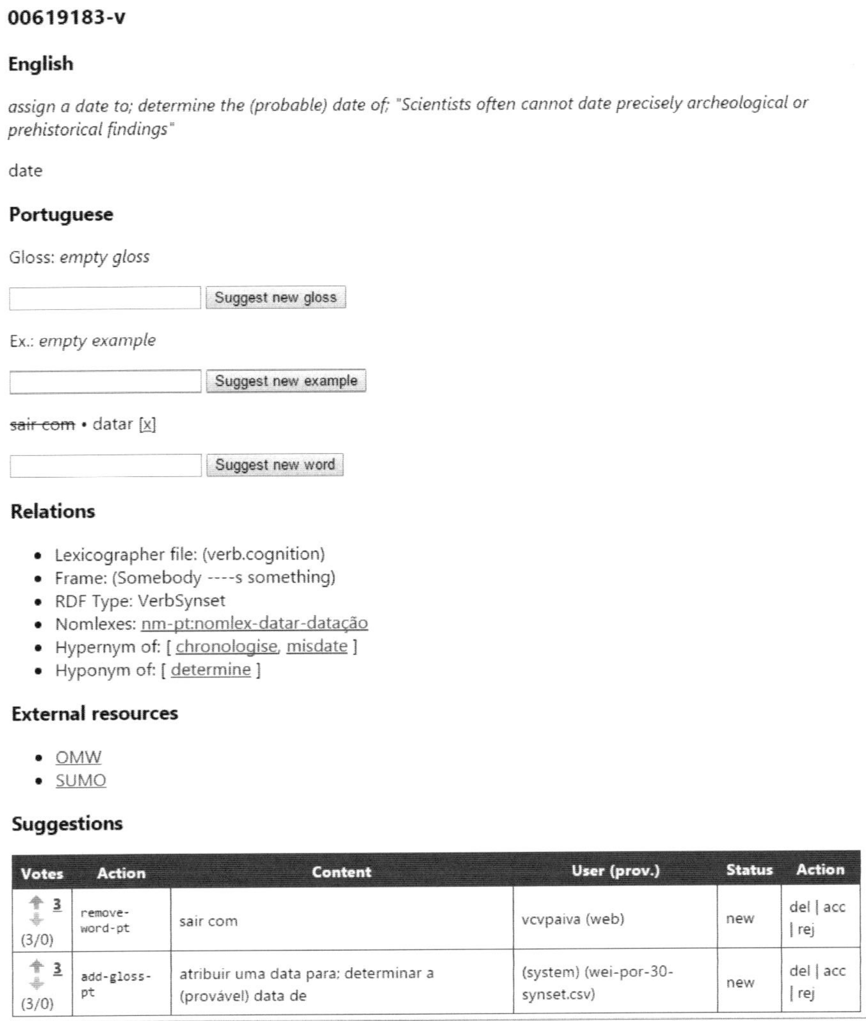

Figure 1: Synset *00619183-v* while voting

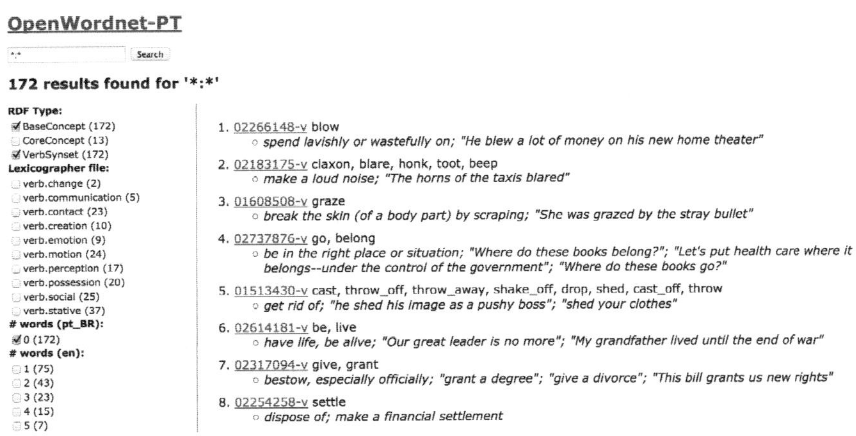

Figure 2: Search for 'All' (*:*) occurrences of BaseConcepts & VerbSynsets

publishing data: (1) data should rely on URIs to identify objects; (2) URIs should be resolvable; (3) semantic information must be returned, using standards such as RDF; and (4) resources in different datasets should be reused through links between those. Linked Data principles and technologies promote the publication of data on the Web and through this effort guides the emergence of the so-called Linguistic Linked Open Data (LLOD) (Chiarcos et al., 2011b) in which resources and datasets are represented in RDF format and linked to each other. Like many other lexical resources, e.g. Onto.PT (Gonçalo Oliveira and Gomes, 2010) and, more recently, Princeton Wordnet (McCrae et al., 2014), OpenWN-PT is primarily distributed as RDF files, following and expanding when necessary, the original mappings proposed by (van Assem et al., 2006). Both the data for the OpenWN-PT and the vocabulary or RDF model (classes and properties) are freely available for download as RDF and OWL files.

Possibly the main motivation for lexical resources to adopt RDF is the first of the Linked Data principles. The use of URIs allows the easy reuse of entities produced by different researchers and groups. When we started the OpenWN-PT project, there was no official RDF distribution of Princeton Wordnet 3.0 available. We developed our mappings to RDF starting from the original data files and proposed patterns for the URIs to name the original Princeton synsets and our own OpenWN-PT synsets. Following the general convention, to avoid conflict of names, we used a domain name that we have control of. The recently created official RDF distribution of Princeton Wordnet [10] could now serve us better without causing any huge impact on our data. That is, without much effort we can start using the new RDF provided by WordNet Princeton linking it to our RDF files, fulfilling some of the general promise of the semantic web. For instance, looking at the first noun synset of Princeton Wordnet, `00001740-n`: regardless of the different URIs people assign to it, one can readily say that all of them represent the same resource. The fragment of Figure 3 shows the declaration of two statements using the `sameAs` property of OWL ontology.

But there are other advantages of the use of RDF, besides providing a universal way to identify entities. RDF allows us to formally specify the properties and classes that we use to model our data. In our case, we had to suggest properties and classes to represent the extensions to the original WordNet data model that allowed us to embed the lexicon of nominalizations NomLex-PT(de Paiva; Livy Real; Alexandre Rademaker; Gerard de Melo, 2014) into OpenWN-PT. The complete specification of our vocabulary is available at the project repository.[11]

We need to improve our new web interface further as, strictly speaking, the interface does not follow the Linked Data principles two and three: although we do provide the RDF data and an SPARQL endpoint for queries, the URLs of the synsets in the interface are not the same nor are they redirected from the URI of our RDF data. Still, while we intend to conform to the principles in the long run, in the mean time we already harvest some of linked data affordances in terms of provenance capture and use.

Provenance can be used for many purposes, including understanding how data was collected, so that it can be meaningfully used; determining ownership; making judgements about information to determine whether to trust it; verifying that the process and steps used to obtain a result comply with given requirements and reproducing how something was generated (Gil and Miles, 2013). We choose to keep track of the evolution of OpenWN-PT using the provenance PROV (Gil and Miles, 2013) data model and make it available in RDF together with the openWN-PT RDF itself. Figure 4 shows our encoding in PROV data model format of a subset of the current possible suggestions that contributors can make to openWN-PT. The contributors are the actors and they are modeled as `foaf:Person` instances. The `prov:Actitivites` are the possible suggestions of modifications in the data and the `prov:Entity` are the items that can be modified in openWN-PT. Although not present in the figure, the PROV data model allows us to also represent the set of suggestions made by one single automated process.

6.1 Testing and Verifying

To investigate how well the *voting mechanism* is coping with the main issues of end users collaborative work, we have tested it for two weeks

[10] `http://wordnet-rdf.princeton.edu`

[11] `http://github.com/arademaker/openWordnet-PT/`

```
prefix wn30pt: <http://arademaker.github.com/wn30-br/instances/>
prefix wn30en: <http://arademaker.github.com/wn30/instances/>
prefix wn30pr: <http://wordnet-rdf.princeton.edu/wn30/>
prefix owl: <http://www.w3.org/2002/07/owl#>

wn30pt:synset-00001740-n owl:sameAs wn30en:synset-00001740-n .
wn30en:synset-00001740-n owl:sameAs wn30pr:00001740-a .
```

Figure 3: Linking resources using RDF

```
wnlog:AddSense     rdf:type prov:Activity .
wnlog:RemoveSense rdf:type prov:Activity .
wn30:WordSense     rdf:type prov:Entity .
wn30:Synset        rdf:type prov:Entity .

:aword rdf:type wn:Word .
:aword wn30:lexicalForm "ente"@pt .
:asense rdf:type wn:WordSense .
:asense wn30:word :aword .

:s1 prov:used wn30pt:synset-00001740-n .
:s1 prov:used :asense .
:s1 rdf:type wnlog:AddSense .
:s1 prov:atTime "2015-04-15"^^xsd:dateTime .
:s1 prov:wasAssociatedWith :a1 .

:s2 prov:used wn30pt:synset-00001740-n .
:s2 prov:used :anothersense .
:s1 prov:atTime "2015-04-15"^^xsd:dateTime .
:s2 rdf:type wnlog:RemoveSense .
:s2 prov:wasAssociatedWith :a1 .

:a1 rdf:type prov:Agent, foaf:Person .
:a1 foaf:name "Alexandre Rademaker" .
:a2 rdf:type prov:Agent, foaf:Person .
:a2 foaf:name "Livy Real" .
```

Figure 4: Preserving provenance information in the RDF

with three Portuguese native speakers who are researchers interested in language. After two weeks of part-time work, over 2400 votes were cast, 2240 suggestions and 110 comments were made, and we identified over 80 new requirements both for functionality and usability—a testimony, we reckon, of the potential of the tool.

These numbers, although preliminary, show how much the new interface helped us to quickly edit and correct existing synsets. Also, we were pleasantly surprised to realize that, during these two weeks, we had two uknown users, not from the team, collaborating with us, by suggesting entries on the new interface. Since we have not announced the suggestions facility at all, so far, this seems to indicate the easiness of use of the tool. Hence we would like to conclude that there is a need for interfaces that allow ordinary users, not only computational linguists to help on the construction, checking, cleaning up and verification of the quality of (lexical) resources. Just like Wikpedia, we hope to tap into this potential good will.

7 Future Work

We still need to complete our main task, the checking of words, glosses and examples from many English synsets and this is our most pressing work. The theoretical and practical decisions on how to integrate the Portuguese senses that are missing from English are major tasks that will require careful thinking, as these choices will have a huge impact not only on the eventual shaping of OpenWN-PT, but also on our other work with Portuguese NLP.

It seems to us clear that the main design choice of creating a lexical resource for Portuguese by automated methods, complemented by manual curation, following Princeton's model, was the right decision. The curation process is not trivial, but it would not be facilitated by starting manually. Neither do we believe that more could be achieved using only automated methods. Keeping the close alignment with Princeton's wordnet is beneficial in many ways, not least of them, because it allows us to connect to the linked open data community and the ontologies it supports. We are still investigating the benefits of using a lexical model such as lemon (Chiarcos et al., 2011a) and of a possible alignment with it.

References

Tim Berners-Lee. 2011. Linked data-design issues. Technical report.

Bluemix. `http://www.bluemix.net`.

Francis Bond and Ryan Foster. 2013. Linking and extending an open multilingual wordnet. In *Proceedings of the 51st Annual Meeting of the Association for Computational Linguistics (Volume 1: Long Papers)*, pages 1352–1362, Sofia, Bulgaria, August. Association for Computational Linguistics.

Adam Meyers Leslie Barrett Ruth Reeves Catherine Macleod, Ralph Grishman. 1998. Nomlex: A lexicon of nominalizations. In *Proceedings of EURALEX'98*, Liege, Belgium.

Christian Chiarcos, Sebastian Hellmann, and Sebastian Nordhoff. 2011a. S.: Towards a linguistic linked open data cloud: The open linguistics working group. *TAL*, pages 245–275.

Christian Chiarcos, Sebastian Hellmann, and Sebastian Nordhoff. 2011b. Towards a linguistic linked open data cloud: The open linguistics working group. *TAL*, 52(3):245–275.

Cloudant. `http://www.cloudant.com`.

Gerard de Melo and Gerhard Weikum. 2009. Towards a universal wordnet by learning from combined evidence. In *Proceedings of the 18th ACM Conference on Information and Knowledge Management (CIKM 2009)*, pages 513–522, New York, NY, USA. ACM.

Valeria de Paiva, Alexandre Rademaker, and Gerard de Melo. 2012. OpenWordNet-PT: An open brazilian wordnet for reasoning. In *Proceedings of 24th International Conference on Computational Linguistics*, COLING (Demo Paper).

Valeria de Paiva, Cláudia Freitas, Livy Real, and Alexandre Rademaker. 2014. Improving the verb lexicon of openwordnet-pt. In Laura Alonso Alemany, Muntsa Padró, Alexandre Rademaker, and Aline Villavicencio, editors, *Proceedings of Workshop on Tools and Resources for Automatically Processing Portuguese and Spanish (ToRPorEsp)*, São Carlos, Brazil, oct. Biblioteca Digital Brasileira de Computao, UFMG, Brazil.

Valeria de Paiva; Livy Real; Alexandre Rademaker; Gerard de Melo. 2014. Nomlex-pt: A lexicon of portuguese nominalizations. *Proceedings of LREC 2014*.

Christiane Fellbaum, editor. 1998. *WordNet: An Electronic Lexical Database (Language, Speech, and Communication)*. The MIT Press.

Cláudia Freitas, Valeria de Paiva, Alexandre Rademaker, Gerard de Melo, Livy Real, and Anne de Araujo Correia da Silva. 2014. Extending a lexicon of portuguese nominalizations with data from corpora. In Jorge Baptista, Nuno Mamede, Sara Candeias, Ivandré Paraboni, Thiago A. S. Pardo, and Maria das Graças Volpe Nunes, editors, *Computational Processing of the Portuguese Language, 11th International Conference, PROPOR 2014*, São Carlos, Brazil, oct. Springer.

Yolanda Gil and Simon Miles. 2013. Prov model primer. Technical report. `http://www.w3.org/TR/prov-primer/`.

Hugo Gonçalo Oliveira and Paulo Gomes. 2010. Onto.PT: Automatic Construction of a Lexical Ontology for Portuguese. In *Proceedings of 5th European Starting AI Researcher Symposium (STAIRS 2010)*, volume 222 of *Frontiers in Artificial Intelligence and Applications*, pages 199–211. IOS Press.

Hugo Gonçalo Oliveira, Diana Santos, Paulo Gomes, and Nuno Seco. 2008. PAPEL: A dictionary-based lexical ontology for Portuguese. In *Proceedings of Computational Processing of the Portuguese Language - 8th International Conference (PROPOR 2008)*, volume 5190 of *LNCS/LNAI*, pages 31–40, Aveiro, Portugal, September. Springer.

Adam Kilgarriff. 1997. I don't believe in word senses. *Computers and the Humanities*, (31):91–113.

John McCrae, Christiane Fellbaum, and Philipp Cimiano. 2014. Publishing and linking wordnet using lemon and rdf. In *Proceedings of the 3rd Workshop on Linked Data in Linguistics*.

NodeJS. `https://nodejs.org`.

Adam Pease and Christiane Fellbaum. 2010. Formal ontology as interlingua: the SUMO and WordNet linking project and global WordNet linking project. In *Ontology and the Lexicon: A Natural Language Processing Perspective*, Studies in Natural Language Processing, chapter 2, pages 25–35. Cambridge University Press.

Alexandre Rademaker, Valeria De Paiva, Gerard de Melo, Livy Maria Real Coelho, and Maira Gatti. 2014. Openwordnet-pt: A project report. In *Proceedings of the 7th Global WordNet Conference*, Tartu, Estonia, jan.

Mark van Assem, Aldo Gangemi, and Guus Schreiber. 2006. RDF/OWL representation of WordNet. W3c working draft, World Wide Web Consortium, June.

Sar-graphs: A Linked Linguistic Knowledge Resource Connecting Facts with Language

Sebastian Krause, Leonhard Hennig, Aleksandra Gabryszak, Feiyu Xu, Hans Uszkoreit
DFKI Language Technology Lab, Berlin, Germany
{skrause,lehe02,alga02,feiyu,uszkoreit}@dfki.de

Abstract

We present *sar-graphs*, a knowledge resource that links semantic relations from factual knowledge graphs to the linguistic patterns with which a language can express instances of these relations. Sar-graphs expand upon existing lexico-semantic resources by modeling syntactic and semantic information at the level of relations, and are hence useful for tasks such as knowledge base population and relation extraction. We present a language-independent method to automatically construct sar-graph instances that is based on distantly supervised relation extraction. We link sar-graphs at the lexical level to BabelNet, WordNet and UBY, and present our ongoing work on pattern- and relation-level linking to FrameNet. An initial dataset of English sar-graphs for 25 relations is made publicly available, together with a Java-based API.

1 Introduction

Knowledge graphs, such as Freebase or YAGO, are networks which contain information about real-world entities and their semantic types, properties and relations. In recent years considerable effort has been invested into constructing these large knowledge bases in academic research, community-driven projects and industrial development (Bollacker et al., 2008; Suchanek et al., 2008; Lehmann et al., 2015). A parallel and in part independent development is the emergence of large-scale lexical-semantic resources, such as BabelNet or UBY, which encode linguistic information about words and their relations (de Melo and Weikum, 2009; Navigli and Ponzetto, 2012; Gurevych et al., 2012). Both types of resources are important contributions to the linguistic linked open data movement, since they address complementary aspects of encyclopedic and linguistic knowledge.

Few to none of the existing resources, however, explicitly link the semantic relations of knowledge graphs to the linguistic patterns, at the level of phrases or sentences, that are used to express these relations in natural language text. Lexical-semantic resources focus on linkage at the level of individual lexical items. For example, BabelNet integrates entity information from Wikipedia with word senses from WordNet, UWN is a multilingual WordNet built from various resources, and UBY integrates several linguistic resources by linking them at the word-sense level. Linguistic knowledge resources that go beyond the level of lexical items are scarce and of limited coverage due to significant investment of human effort and expertise required for their construction. Among these are FrameNet (Baker et al., 1998), which provides fine-grained semantic relations of predicates and their arguments, and VerbNet (Schuler, 2005), which models verb-class specific syntactic and semantic preferences. What is missing, therefore, is a large-scale, preferably automatically constructed linguistic resource that links language expressions at the phrase or sentence level to the semantic relations of knowledge bases, as well as to existing terminological resources. Such a repository would be very useful for many information extraction tasks, e.g., for relation extraction and knowledge base population.

We aim to fill this gap with a resource whose structure we define in Section 2. Instances of this resource are *graphs of semantically-associated relations*, which we refer to by the name *sar-graphs*. We believe that sar-graphs are examples for a new type of knowledge repository, *language graphs*, as they represent the linguistic patterns for the relations contained in a knowledge graph. A language graph can be thought of as a bridge between

Proceedings of the 4th Workshop on Linked Data in Linguistics (LDL-2015), pages 30–38,
Beijing, China, July 31, 2015.

the language and the facts encoded in a knowledge graph, a bridge that characterizes the ways in which a language can express instances of relations. Our contributions in this paper are as follows:

- We present a model for *sar-graphs*, a resource of linked linguistic patterns which are used to express factual information from knowledge graphs in natural language text. We model these patterns at a fine-grained lexico-syntactic and semantic level (Section 2).
- We describe the word-level linking of sar-graph patterns to existing lexical-semantic resources (BabelNet, WordNet, and UBY; Section 3)
- We discuss our ongoing work of linking sar-graphs at the pattern and relation level to FrameNet (Section 4)
- We describe a language-independent, distantly supervised approach for automatically constructing sar-graph instances, and present a first published and linked dataset of English sar-graphs for 25 Freebase relations (Section 5)

2 Sar-graphs: A linguistic knowledge resource

Sar-graphs (Uszkoreit and Xu, 2013) extend the current range of knowledge graphs, which represent factual, relational and common-sense information for one or more languages, with linguistic variants of how semantic relations between real-world entities are expressed in natural language.

Definition Sar-graphs are directed multigraphs containing linguistic knowledge at the syntactic and lexical semantic level. A sar-graph is a tuple

$$G_{r,l} = (V, E, f, A_f, \Sigma_f),$$

where V is the set of vertices and E is the set of edges. The labeling function f associates both vertices and edges with sets of features (i.e., attribute-value pairs):

$$f : V \cup E \mapsto \mathcal{P}(A_f \times \Sigma_f)$$

where

- $\mathcal{P}(\cdot)$ constructs a powerset,
- A_f is the set of attributes (i.e., attribute names) which vertices and edges may have, and
- Σ_f is the value alphabet of the features, i.e., the set of possible attribute values for all attributes.

The function of sar-graphs is to represent the linguistic constructions a language l provides for referring to instances of r. A vertex $v \in V$ corresponds to either a word in such a construction, or an argument of the relation. The features assigned to a vertex via the labeling function f provide information about lexico-syntactic aspects (*word form* and *lemma*, *word class*), and lexical semantics (*word sense*), or semantic attributes (*global entity identifier*, *entity type*, *semantic role in the target relation*). They may also provide statistical and meta information (e.g., *frequency*). The linguistic constructions are modeled as sub-trees of dependency-graph representations of sentences. We will refer to these trees as *dependency structures* or *dependency constructions*. Each structure typically describes one particular way to express relation r in language l. Edges $e \in E$ are consequently labeled with dependency tags, in addition to, e.g., frequency information.

A given graph instance is specific to a language l and target relation r. In general, r links $n \geq 2$ entities. An example relation is *marriage*, connecting two spouses to one another, and optionally to the location and date of their wedding, as well as to their date of divorce:

$$r_{mar.}(\textsc{Spouse1}, \textsc{Spouse2}, \textsc{Ceremony}, \textsc{From}, \textsc{To}).$$

If a given language l only provides a single construction to express an instance of r, then the dependency structure of this construction forms the entire sar-graph. But if the language offers alternatives to this construction, i.e., paraphrases, their dependency structures are also added to the sar-graph. They are connected in such a way that all vertices labeled by the same argument name are merged, i.e., lexical specifics like word form, lemma, class, etc. are dropped from the vertices corresponding to the semantic arguments of the target relation. The granularity of such a dependency-structure merge is however not fixed and can be adapted to application needs.

Figure 1 presents a sar-graph for five English constructions with mentions of the *marriage* relation. The graph covers the target relation relevant parts of the individual mentions, assembled stepwise in a bottom-up fashion. Consider the two sentences in the top-left corner of the figure:

Example 1

- *I met Eve's husband Jack.*
- *Lucy and Peter are married since 2011.*

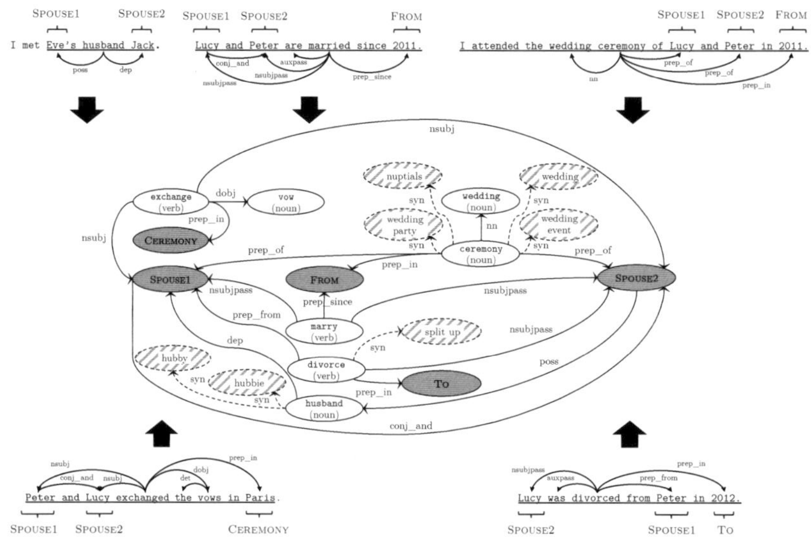

Figure 1: Example sar-graph for the *marriage* relation, constructed using the dependency patterns extracted from the sentences shown in the figure. Dashed vertices and edges represent additional graph elements obtained by linking lexical vertices to BabelNet.

From the dependency parse trees of these sentences, we can extract two graphs that connect the relation's arguments. The first sentence lists the spouses with a possessive construction, the second sentence using a conjunction. In addition, the second sentence provides the marriage date. The graph we extract from the latter sentence hence includes the dependency arcs *nsubjpass* and *prep_since*, as well as the node for the content word *marry*. We connect the two extracted structures by their shared semantic arguments, namely, SPOUSE1 and SPOUSE2. As a result, the graph in Figure 1 contains a path from SPOUSE1 to SPOUSE2 via the node *husband* for sentence (1), and an edge *conj_and* from SPOUSE1 to SPOUSE2 for sentence (2). The dependency relations connecting the FROM argument yield the remainder of the sar-graph.

The remaining three sentences from the figure provide alternative linguistic constructions, as well as the additional arguments CEREMONY and TO. The graph includes the paraphrases *exchange vows*, *wedding ceremony of*, and *was divorced from*. Note that both sentence (2) and (4) utilize a *conj_and* to connect the SPOUSES. The sar-graph includes this information as a single edge, but we can encode the frequency information as an edge attribute.

Less explicit relation mentions A key property of sar-graphs is that they store linguistic structures with varying degrees of explicitness wrt. to the underlying semantic relations. Constructions that refer to some part or aspect of the relation would normally be seen as sufficient evidence of an instance even if there could be contexts in which this implication is canceled:

Example 2

- *Joan and Edward exchanged rings in 2011.*
- *Joan and Edward exchanged rings during the rehearsal of the ceremony.*

Other constructions refer to relations that entail the target relations without being part of it:

Example 3

- *Joan and Edward celebrated their 12th wedding anniversary.*
- *Joan and Edward got divorced in 2011.*

3 Word-level linking

We link sar-graphs to existing linguistic linked open data (LOD) resources on the lexical level by mapping content word vertices to the lexical semantic resource BabelNet (Navigli and Ponzetto, 2012), and via BabelNet to WordNet and UBY-OmegaWiki. BabelNet is a large-scale multilingual semantic network automatically constructed from resources such as Wikipedia and WordNet. Its core components are Babel synsets, which are

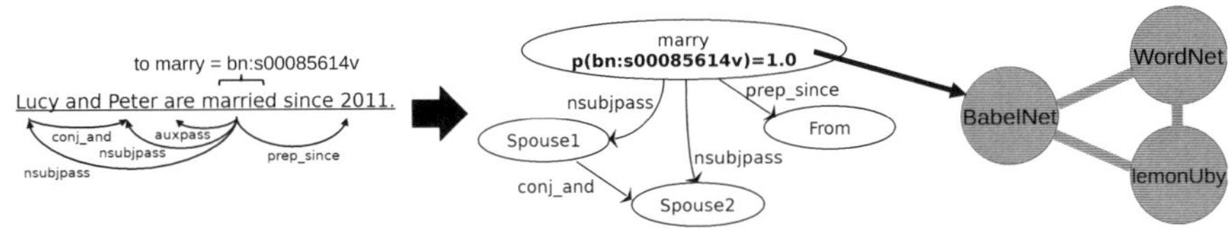

Figure 2: A minimal sar-graph disambiguation example, consisting of a single pattern, where the lexical vertex *marry* is disambiguated and linked to BabelNet, UBY, and WordNet.

sets of multilingual synonyms. Each Babel synset is related to other Babel synsets via semantic relations such as hypernymy, meronymy and semantic relatedness. BabelNet contains roughly 13M synsets, 117M lexicalizations and 354M relation instances.

Besides connecting sar-graphs to the linguistic LOD cloud, this mapping allows us to augment the lexico-syntactic and semantic information specified in sar-graphs with lexical semantic knowledge from the linked resources. In particular, we introduce new vertices for synonyms, and add new edges based on the lexical semantic relations specified in BabelNet. In Figure 1, these additional graph elements are represented as dashed vertices and edges.

To link sar-graph vertices to Babelnet, we disambiguate content words in our pattern extraction pipeline (see Section 5), using the graph-based approach described by Moro et al. (2014). The disambiguation is performed on a per-sentence basis, considering all content words in the sentence as potentially ambiguous mentions if they correspond to at least one candidate meaning in BabelNet. This includes multi-token sequences containing at least one noun. The candidate senses (synset identifiers) of all mentions in a sentence are linked to each other via their BabelNet relations to create a graph. The approach then iteratively prunes low-probability candidate senses from the graph to select the synset assignment that maximizes the semantic agreement within a given sentence. Once we have found this disambiguation assignment, we can use BabelNet's existing synset mappings to link each mention to its corresponding synsets in UBY-OmegaWiki and in the original Princeton WordNet. Figure 2 illustrates the word-level linking.

After extracting a dependency pattern from a given sentence, we store the synset assignments as a property for each content word vertex of the pattern. In the final, merged sar-graph, each content word vertex is hence associated with a distribution over synset assignments, since the same pattern may occur in multiple source sentences, with potentially different local disambiguation decisions.

4 Alignment to FrameNet

In addition to the straightforward sense-level linking of sar-graphs to thesauri, we aim to establish connections at more abstract information layers, e.g., to valency lexicons. In this section, we present our ongoing efforts for aligning sar-graphs with FrameNet at the level of phrases and relations.

FrameNet The Berkeley FrameNet Project (Baker et al., 1998; Ruppenhofer et al., 2006) has created a lexical resource for English that documents the range of semantic and syntactic combinatorial possibilities of words and their senses. FrameNet consists of schematic representations of situations (called *frames*), e.g., the frame *win_prize* describes an awarding situation with *frame elements* (FE), i.e., semantic roles, like COMPETITOR, PRIZE, COMPETITION etc.

A pair of a word and a frame forms a *lexical unit* (LU), similar to a particular word sense in a thesaurus. LUs are connected to *lexical entries* (LEs), which capture the valency patterns of frames, providing information about FEs and their phrase types and grammatical functions in relation to the LUs. In total, the FrameNet release 1.5 contains 1019 frames, 9385 lemmas, 11829 lexical units and more than 170,000 annotated sentences.

Comparison to sar-graphs Sar-graphs resemble frames in many aspects, e.g., both define semantic roles for target concepts and provide detailed valency information for linguistic constructions referring to the concept. Table 1 compares some properties of the two resources.

Sar-graphs model relations derived from factual knowledge bases like DBpedia (Lehmann et al., 2015), whereas FrameNet is based on the

FrameNet: A frame ...	A **sar-graph** ...
... is based on the linguistic theory of frame semantics.	... is defined by a relation in a world-knowledge database.
... groups expressions implicating a situational concept by subsumption.	... groups linguistic structures expressing or implying a relation.
... groups lemmas and their valency patterns.	... groups phrase patterns.
... can have relations to other frames.	... is not explicitly connected to other sar-graphs.

Table 1: Comparison of FrameNet frames to sar-graphs on a conceptual level.

linguistic theory of *frame semantics* (Fillmore, 1976). This theory assumes that human cognitive processing involves an inventory of explicit schemata for classifying, structuring and interpreting experiences. Consequently, FrameNet contains a number of very generic frames (e.g., *forming_relationships*) that have no explicit equivalent in a sar-graph relation. The database-driven sar-graphs also specify fewer semantic roles than frames typically do, covering mainly the most important aspects of a relational concept from a knowledge-base population perspective. For example, the sar-graph for *marriage* lists arguments for the SPOUSES, LOCATION and DATE of the wedding ceremony as well as a DIVORCEDATE, while the related frame *forming_relationships* additionally covers, e.g., an EXPLANATION (divorce reason, etc.) and an ITERATION counter (for the relationships of a person).

Above that, FrameNet specifies relations between frames (*inheritance*, *subframe*, *perspective on*, *using*, *causative of*, *inchoative of*, *see also*) and connects in this way also the lexical units evoking the related frames. For example, frames *commerce_buy* and *commerce_sell* represent perspectives on the frame *commerce_good_transfer*, and link by the same relation the verbs `to sell` and `to buy`. Sar-graphs are currently not linked to one another.

Another difference is the relationship between lexical items and their corresponding frames/sar-graph relations. LUs in FrameNet imply frames by subsumption, e.g., `to befriend` and `to divorce` are subsumed by *forming_relationships*. In comparison, sar-graphs cluster both expressions that directly refer to instances of the target relation (e.g., `to wed` for *marriage*) and those that only entail them (e.g., `to divorce` for *marriage*). This entailment is, in turn, partly represented in FrameNet via frame-to-frame relations like *inheritance*, *cause* and *perspective*.

The data perspective Not only do frames and sar-graphs model different (but related) aspects of the same semantic concepts, they also cover different sets of lexical items, i.e. lemmas with corresponding senses and valency patterns. For example, FrameNet 1.5 neither contains the idiomatic phrase `exchange vows` nor the lemma `remarry` for the *forming_relationships* frame, in contrast to the *marriage* sar-graph; while the sar-graph does not contain all the valency patterns of the LU `widow` which the corresponding frame provides.

A statistical analysis shows that the *marriage* sar-graph and the frames *forming_relationships, personal_relationship, social_connection*, and *relation_between_individuals* share only 7% of their lemmas. The sar-graph adds 62% of the total number of lemmas, FrameNet the remaining 31%. For the *acquisition* relation between companies, values are similar: 6% shared, 79% additional lemmas in the sar-graph, and 15% of the relevant lemmas are only contained in FrameNet.

Linking sar-graphs to FrameNet The similarities between FrameNet and sar-graphs can be used to link the two resources at the level of:

- lexical items (or senses),
- valency patterns and phrase patterns,
- frames and sar-graph relations.

The linking of sar-graphs on the lemma level was already presented in Section 3; in the following we briefly outline some ideas for the (semi-) automatic alignment on the other two levels.

A first linking approach can be to define a similarity metric between sar-graph phrase patterns and FrameNet valency patterns. The metric might include a wide range of semantic and syntactic features of the pattern elements, such as lemma, part of speech, phrase type, grammatical function, and conceptual roles. As both resources work with different label inventories, this would require a manual mapping step on the conceptual level.

	FrameNet	SarGraph
lemma	`marry`	`marry`
part of speech	verb	verb, past tense
semantic role	PARTNER1	SPOUSE1
role filler	nominal phrase	person mention
gramm. function	external argument	nominal subject
semantic role	PARTNER2	SPOUSE2
role filler	nominal phrase	person mention
gramm. function	object	direct object
semantic role	TIME	DATE
role filler	prep. phrase	date mention
gramm. function	dependent	prep. modifier

Table 2: Example for pattern-level mapping between FrameNet (a valence pattern of LU *marry.v*) and sar-graphs (pattern *marriage*#5088).

However, the effort for this step would be reasonably low because the overall number of labels is relatively small. Table 2 presents an example mapping for patterns covering phrases like "SPOUSE1 `married` SPOUSE2 `on` DATE".

The described approach can be extended by incorporating annotated sentences from FrameNet which match particular sar-graph patterns, thereby connecting these to the sentences' corresponding valency patterns. The pattern matching can be done automatically, using the same algorithm as when applying patterns to extract novel relation instances from text. Because there are cases where such a match might be misleading (e.g., for long sentences with several mentioned relations), additionally applying a similarity function seems reasonable.

Linking sar-graphs to valency patterns in FrameNet also provides connections on the relation-to-frame level, as every valency pattern is derived from a lexical unit associated with a unique frame. Because of the conceptual differences between FrameNet and sar-graphs, the mapping of frames to relations is not one-to-one but rather a many-to-many linking. For example, the relation *marriage* might equally likely be mapped to one of the more abstract frames *forming_relationships* and *personal_relationship*. The frame *personal_relationships* is related to *personal_relationship* by the inter-frame relation *inchoative of*. The frame *leadership* can be linked to the sar-graph relations *organization leadership* and *organization membership*, since the last one includes also patterns with the lemma `lead` or `leader`, which imply the membership in some group.

Relation	$\|Patterns\|$	$\|V\|$	$\|E\|$
award honor	510	303	876
award nomination	392	369	1,091
country of nationality	560	424	1,265
education	270	233	631
marriage	451	193	584
person alternate name	542	717	1,960
person birth	151	124	319
person death	306	159	425
person parent	387	157	589
person religion	142	196	420
place lived	329	445	1,065
sibling relationship	140	103	260
acquisition	224	268	676
business operation	264	416	876
company end	465	714	1,909
company product rel.	257	421	929
employment tenure	226	131	374
foundation	397	231	708
headquarters	273	220	570
org. alternate name	280	283	720
organization leadership	547	213	717
organization membership	291	262	718
organization relationship	303	317	862
organization type	264	566	1,168
sponsorship	336	523	1,298
Total	**8,307**	**7,988**	**21,010**

Table 3: Dataset statistics

5 Sar-graph dataset

We generated a dataset of sar-graphs for 25 relations from the domains of biographical, awards and business information, with English as the target language. The dataset is available at `http://sargraph.dfki.de`. In this section, we briefly describe some implementation details of the generation process, and present key dataset statistics.

Sar-graph construction We construct sar-graphs using an approach that is language- and relation-independent, and relies solely on the availability of a set of seed relation instances from an existing knowledge base (KB). As described in Section 2, each sar-graph is the result of merging a set of dependency constructions, or patterns. We obtain these dependency constructions by implementing a distantly supervised pattern extraction approach (Mintz et al., 2009; Krause et al., 2012; Gerber and Ngomo, 2014).

We use *Freebase* (Bollacker et al., 2008) as our KB, and select relations of arity $2 \leq n \leq 5$, based on their coverage in Freebase (see Table 3). The selection includes kinship relations (e.g., *mar-*

```xml
<?xml version="1.0" encoding="utf-8"?>
<rdf:RDF xmlns:rdf="http://www.w3.org/1999/02/22-rdf-syntax-ns#">
<lemon:Lexicon rdf:about="http://dare.dfki.de/lemon/lexicon"
               xmlns:lemon="http://www.monnet-project.eu/lemon#">
<lemon:language>en
<lemon:entry>
  <lemon:LexicalEntry rdf:about="http://dare.dfki.de/lemon/lexicon/marriage_12024">
    <lemon:canonicalForm>
      <lemon:Form rdf:about="http://dare.dfki.de/lemon/lexicon/marriage_12024#form">
        <lemon:writtenRep xml:lang="en">marry\VBN C_person C_person in\IN C_location
    <lemon:phraseRoot>
      <lemon:Node rdf:about="http://dare.dfki.de/lemon/lexicon/marriage_12024#phraseRoot">
        <root xmlns="http://dare.dfki.de/lemon/ontology#">
          <lemon:Node rdf:about="http://dare.dfki.de/lemon/lexicon/marriage_12024#node1">
            <prep>
              <lemon:Node rdf:about="http://dare.dfki.de/lemon/lexicon/marriage_12024#node4">
                <pobj>
                  ...
                <lemon:leaf>
                  ...
            <lemon:leaf>
              <lemon:Component rdf:about="http://dare.dfki.de/lemon/lexicon/marriage_12024#comp1">
                <lemon:element>
                  <lemon:LexicalEntry rdf:about="http://dare.dfki.de/lemon/lexicon/marry#12024">
                    <lemon:sense>
                      <lemon:LexicalSense rdf:about="http://babelnet.org/synset?word=bn:00090675v"/>
                    <lemon:canonicalForm>
                      <lemon:Form rdf:about="http://dare.dfki.de/lemon/lexicon/marry#form_12024">
                        <lemon:writtenRep xml:lang="en">marry
                    ...
            ...
  <lemon:synBehavior>
    <lemon:Frame rdf:about="http://dare.dfki.de/lemon/lexicon/marriage_12024#frame">
      <person rdf:resource="http://dare.dfki.de/lemon/lexicon/marriage_12024#C_person"
              xmlns="http://dare.dfki.de/lemon/ontology#"/>
      ...
...
```

Figure 3: Excerpt from the sar-graph pattern for the phrase "SPOUSE1 *and* SPOUSE2 *got married in* LOCATION on DATE." In Lemon format; closing tags omitted for brevity.

riage, *parent-child*, *siblings*) and biographical information (*person birth/death*), but also typical inter-business relations and properties of companies (e.g., *acquisition*, *business operation*, *headquarters*). Using Freebase' query API, we retrieved a total of 223K seed instances for the 25 target relations.

The seeds are converted to web search engine queries to generate a text corpus containing mentions of the seeds. We collected a total of 2M relevant documents, which were preprocessed using a standard NLP pipeline for sentence segmentation, tokenization, named entity recognition and linking, lemmatization, part-of-speech tagging and word sense disambiguation. We also applied a dependency parser to annotate sentences with Stanford dependency relations. After preprocessing, we discarded duplicate sentences, and sentences that did not contain mentions of the seed relation instances.

From the remaining 1M unique sentences, we extracted 600K distinct dependency patterns by finding the minimum spanning tree covering the arguments of a given seed instance. To reduce the number of low-quality patterns, a side effect of the distantly supervised learning scheme, we implemented the filtering strategies proposed by Moro et al. (2013). These strategies compute confidence metrics based on pattern distribution statistics and on the semantic coherence of a pattern's content words. Patterns with low confidence scores are discarded. To create a sar-graph instance, we then merge the patterns based on their shared relation argument vertices (see Figure 1). Sar-graph instances, patterns, and vertices are assigned unique ids to support efficient lookup.

Dataset statistics and format Table 3 summarizes key statistics of the dataset. The curated sar-graphs range in size from 140–560 unique patterns. The largest sar-graph, for the *person alternate name* relation, contains 1960 edges and 717 vertices. The smallest sar-graph was constructed for the *sibling* relation, it contains 260 edges and 103 vertices, derived from 140 dependency patterns. Overall, the dataset contains approximately 8,300 unique patterns. While this experimental dataset is not as large as other linguistic LOD resources, we emphasize that the construction of additional sar-graph instances, e.g., for other relations or a different language, is a fully automatic process given a set of seed relation instances.

We provide the dataset in a custom, XML-based format, and in the semantic web dialect *Lemon*.[1] Lemon was originally designed for modeling dic-

[1] http://www.lemon-model.net/

tionaries and lexicons. It builds on RDF and provides facilities for expressing lexicon-relevant aspects of a resource, e.g., lexical items with different forms and senses. Albeit Lemon is not a perfect fit for representing sar-graphs and their individual pattern elements, it still constitutes a good first step for establishing sar-graphs as part of the linguistic linked open data cloud.

Figure 3 shows an example pattern in Lemon format. Patterns are realized via Lemon *lexicon entries*, where each such entry has an attached phrase root whose child nodes contain information about the syntactic and lexical elements of the pattern.

Java-based API We provide a Java-based API which simplifies loading, processing, and storing sar-graphs. One exemplary API feature are materialized views, which present the sar-graph data in the respective most informative way to an application, as with different tasks and goals, varying aspects of a sar-graph may become relevant.

6 Related Work

In comparison to well-known knowledge bases such as YAGO (Suchanek et al., 2008), DBpedia (Lehmann et al., 2015), Freebase (Bollacker et al., 2008), or the recent Google Knowledge Vault (Dong et al., 2014), sar-graphs are not a database of facts or events, but rather a repository of linguistic expressions of these. The acquisition of sar-graph elements is related to pattern discovery approaches developed in traditional schema-based IE systems, e.g., NELL (Mitchell et al., 2015) or PROSPERA (Nakashole et al., 2011), meaning that sar-graphs can be directly applied to free texts for enlarging a structured repository of knowledge.

Many linguistic resources, such as WordNet (Fellbaum, 1998), FrameNet (Baker et al., 1998), and VerbNet (Schuler, 2005) already existed before the recent development of large knowledge bases. These resources model the semantics of languages at the word or syntactic level, without an explicit link to real world facts. Most of them were manually created and are relatively small. WordNet captures lexical semantic relations between individual words, such as synonymy, homonymy, and antonymy. FrameNet focuses on fine-grained semantic relations of predicates and their arguments. VerbNet is a lexicon that maps verbs to predefined classes which define the syntactic and semantic preferences of the verb. In contrast to these resources, sar-graphs are data-driven, constructed automatically, and incorporate statistical information about relations and their arguments. Therefore, sar-graphs complement these manually constructed linguistic resources.

There is also increasing research in creating large-scale linguistic resources, e.g., BabelNet (Navigli and Ponzetto, 2012), ConceptNet (Speer and Havasi, 2013) and UBY (Gurevych et al., 2012) automatically. Many of these are built on top of existing resources like WordNet, Wiktionary and Wikipedia, e.g., BabelNet merges Wikipedia concepts including entities with word senses from WordNet. ConceptNet is a semantic network encoding common-sense knowledge and merging information from various sources such as WordNet, Wiktionary, Wikipedia and ReVerb. In comparison to sar-graphs, it contains no explicit linguistic knowledge like syntactic or word-sense information assigned to the content elements, and the semantic relations among concepts are not fixed to an ontology or schema. UBY combines and aligns several lexico-semantic resources, and provides a standardized representation via the Lexical Markup Framework.

7 Conclusion

We presented sar-graphs, a linguistic resource linking semantic relations from knowledge graphs to their associated natural language expressions. Sar-graphs can be automatically constructed for any target language and relation in a distantly supervised fashion, i.e. given only a set of seed relation instances from an existing knowledge graph, and a text corpus. We publish an initial dataset which contains sar-graphs for 25 Freebase relations, spanning the domains of biographical, award, and business information. The released sar-graphs are linked at the lexical level to BabelNet, WordNet and UBY, and are made available in Lemon-RDF and a custom XML-based format at `http://sargraph.dfki.de`.

For future releases of the sar-graph dataset, we intend to publish the non-curated part of the pattern data, and to provide more detailed information about the source of linguistic expressions (i.e., to expand the public data with source sentences and seed facts). Furthermore, we will continue our work on linking sar-graphs to FrameNet, in particular we will focus on semi-automatic phrase-level linking, for which we have outlined some early ideas in this paper. We also plan to expand the dataset to more relations and additional languages.

Acknowledgments

This research was partially supported by the German Federal Ministry of Education and Research (BMBF) through the projects ALL SIDES (01IW14002) and BBDC (01IS14013E), by the German Federal Ministry of Economics and Energy (BMWi) through the projects SDW (01MD15010A) and SD4M (01MD15007B), and by Google through a Focused Research Award granted in July 2013. We would also like to thank Min Fang and Hong Li for their help with the implementation.

References

C. F. Baker, C. J. Fillmore, and J. B. Lowe. 1998. The Berkeley FrameNet Project. In *Proc. of ACL-COLING*, pages 86–90.

K. Bollacker, C. Evans, P. Paritosh, T. Sturge, and J. Taylor. 2008. Freebase: A Collaboratively Created Graph Database for Structuring Human Knowledge. In *Proc. of SIGMOD*, pages 1247–1250.

G. de Melo and G. Weikum. 2009. Towards a Universal Wordnet by Learning from Combined Evidence. In *Proc. of CIKM*, pages 513–522.

X. Dong, E. Gabrilovich, G. Heitz, W. Horn, N. Lao, K. Murphy, T. Strohmann, S. Sun, and W. Zhang. 2014. Knowledge Vault: A Web-scale Approach to Probabilistic Knowledge Fusion. In *Proc. of SIGKDD*, pages 601–610.

Ch. Fellbaum, editor. 1998. *WordNet: An Electronic Lexical Database*. MIT Press, Cambridge, MA.

C. J. Fillmore. 1976. Frame semantics and the nature of language. *Annals of the New York Academy of Sciences: Conference on the Origin and Development of Language and Speech*, 280(1):20–32.

Daniel Gerber and Axel-Cyrille Ngonga Ngomo. 2014. From RDF to natural language and back. In *Towards the Multilingual Semantic Web*. Springer Berlin Heidelberg.

I. Gurevych, J. Eckle-Kohler, S. Hartmann, M. Matuschek, Ch. M. Meyer, and Ch. Wirth. 2012. Uby: A Large-scale Unified Lexical-semantic Resource Based on LMF. In *Proc. of EACL*, pages 580–590.

S. Krause, H. Li, H. Uszkoreit, and F. Xu. 2012. Large-Scale Learning of Relation-Extraction Rules with Distant Supervision from the Web. In *Proc. of ISWC*, pages 263–278.

J. Lehmann, R. Isele, M. Jakob, A. Jentzsch, D. Kontokostas, P. N. Mendes, S. Hellmann, M. Morsey, P. van Kleef, S. Auer, and Ch. Bizer. 2015. DBpedia - A Large-scale, Multilingual Knowledge Base Extracted from Wikipedia. *Semantic Web Journal*, 6(2):167–195.

M. Mintz, S. Bills, R. Snow, and D. Jurafsky. 2009. Distant supervision for relation extraction without labeled data. In *Proc. of ACL/IJCNLP*, pages 1003–1011.

T. Mitchell, W. Cohen, E. Hruschka, P. Talukdar, J. Betteridge, A. Carlson, B. Dalvi, M. Gardner, B. Kisiel, J. Krishnamurthy, N. Lao, K. Mazaitis, T. Mohamed, N. Nakashole, E. Platanios, A. Ritter, M. Samadi, B. Settles, R. Wang, D. Wijaya, A. Gupta, X. Chen, A. Saparov, M. Greaves, and J. Welling. 2015. Never-ending learning. In *Proc. of AAAI*.

A. Moro, H. Li, S. Krause, F. Xu, R. Navigli, and H. Uszkoreit. 2013. Semantic Rule Filtering for Web-Scale Relation Extraction. In *Proc. of ISWC*, pages 347–362.

A. Moro, A. Raganato, and R. Navigli. 2014. Entity linking meets word sense disambiguation: A unified approach. *TACL*, 2:231–244.

N. Nakashole, M. Theobald, and G. Weikum. 2011. Scalable Knowledge Harvesting with High Precision and High Recall. In *Proc. of WSDM*, pages 227–236.

R. Navigli and S. P. Ponzetto. 2012. Babelnet: The automatic construction, evaluation and application of a wide-coverage multilingual semantic network. *Artificial Intelligence*, 193:217–250.

J. Ruppenhofer, M. Ellsworth, M. Petruck, C. Johnson, and J. Scheffczyk. 2006. *FrameNet II: Extended Theory and Practice*. International Computer Science Institute, Berkeley, California.

K. K. Schuler. 2005. *Verbnet: A Broad-coverage, Comprehensive Verb Lexicon*. Ph.D. thesis, University of Pennsylvania, Philadelphia, PA, USA.

R. Speer and C. Havasi. 2013. ConceptNet 5: A Large Semantic Network for Relational Knowledge. In *The People's Web Meets NLP*, pages 161–176. Springer Berlin Heidelberg.

F. M. Suchanek, G. Kasneci, and G. Weikum. 2008. YAGO: A Large Ontology from Wikipedia and WordNet. *Web Semantics: Science, Services and Agents on the World Wide Web*, 6(3):203–217.

H. Uszkoreit and F. Xu. 2013. From Strings to Things – Sar-Graphs: A New Type of Resource for Connecting Knowledge and Language. In *Proc. of WS on NLP and DBpedia*.

Reconciling Heterogeneous Descriptions of Language Resources

John P. McCrae, Philipp Cimiano
CIT-EC, Bielefeld University
Bielefeld, Germany
{jmccrae, cimiano}@cit-ec.uni-bielefeld.de

Luca Matteis, Roberto Navigli
University of Rome, La Sapienza
Rome, Italy
{matteis, navigli}@di.uniroma1.it

Victor Rodríguez Doncel, Daniel Vila-Suero
Jorge Gracia
Universidad Politécnica de Madrid
Madrid, Spain
{vrodriguez, dvila, jgracia}@fi.upm.es

Andrejs Abele, Gabriela Vulcu
Paul Buitelaar
Insight Centre, National University of Ireland
Galway, Ireland
{andrejs.abele, gabriela.vulcu,
paul.buitelaar}@insight-centre.org

Abstract

Language resources are a cornerstone of linguistic research and for the development of natural language processing tools, but the discovery of relevant resources remains a challenging task. This is due to the fact that relevant metadata records are spread among different repositories and it is currently impossible to query all these repositories in an integrated fashion, as they use different data models and vocabularies. In this paper we present a first attempt to collect and harmonize the metadata of different repositories, thus making them queriable and browsable in an integrated way. We make use of RDF and linked data technologies for this and provide a first level of harmonization of the vocabularies used in the different resources by mapping them to standard RDF vocabularies including Dublin Core and DCAT. Further, we present an approach that relies on NLP and in particular word sense disambiguation techniques to harmonize resources by mapping values of attributes – such as the type, license or intended use of a resource – into normalized values. Finally, as there are duplicate entries within the same repository as well as across different repositories, we also report results of detection of these duplicates.

1 Introduction

Language resources are the cornerstone of linguistic research as well as of computational linguistics. Within NLP, for instance, most tools developed require a corpus to be trained (e.g. language models, statistical taggers, statistical parsers, and statistical machine translation systems) or they require lexico-semantic resources as background knowledge to perform some task (e.g. word sense disambiguation). As the number of language resources available keeps growing, the task of discovering and finding resources that are pertinent to a particular task becomes increasingly difficult. While there are a number of repositories that collect and index metadata of language resources, such as META-SHARE (Federmann et al., 2012), CLARIN (Broeder et al., 2010), LRE-Map (Calzolari et al., 2012), Datahub.io[1] and OLAC (Simons and Bird, 2003), they do not provide a complete solution to the discovery problem for two reasons. First, integrated search over all these different repositories is not possible, as they use different data models, different vocabularies and expose different interfaces and APIs. Second, these repositories must strike a balance between quality and coverage, either opting for coverage at the expense of quality of metadata, or *vice versa*.

When collecting metadata from multiple resources, we understand that there are two principal challenges: property harmonization and duplication detection. Harmonization is the challenge of verifying that there is not only structural and syntactic interoperability between the resources in that they use the same property, for example Dublin Core's language property, but also that they use the same value. For example, the following values of the language property are likely to be equivalent: "French", "Modern French", "français", "fr", "fra" and "fre". It is difficult to write queries on a dataset if every property has many equivalent values and thus it is essential to use a single representation. Secondly, we wish to

[1] http://datahub.io/

Proceedings of the 4th Workshop on Linked Data in Linguistics (LDL-2015), pages 39–48,
Beijing, China, July 31, 2015.

detect duplicates that occur either due to the original representation or from multiple sources. It is clear that if a large number of records in fact describe the same resource then queries for that resource will return too many resources that may lead to errors (or annoyance) for users. For example, the "Universal Declaration of Human Rights" is available in 444 languages[2] and listing each translation as a single resource (as the CLARIN VLO does) does not correctly capture the nature of the resource. Furthermore, these resources may not match some queries, such as for example 'resources in more than one language', and as such it is preferable to merge these individual records into a single complex record.

As the main contribution of this paper, we present the methods used to harmonize data across repositories. Due to the different kinds of values and target taxonomies chosen for each property, these methods vary but all are based on state-of-the-art NLP techniques, including word sense disambiguation, and make major improvements to the data quality of our metadata records. Second, we show indeed that duplicate metadata records are pervasive and that they occur both within and across repositories. We then present a simple yet effective approach to detect duplicates within and across repositories.

The paper is structured as follows: we give an overview of work related to harmonization of data as well as an overview of existing metadata repositories for linguistic data in Section 2. We describe our metadata collection and schema matching strategy in Section 3. We describe our techniques for metadata harmonization in Section 4. We describe our methods for duplication detection in Section 5. The performance of the different techniques is reported in each of these sections. We discuss our methodology and approach from a wider point of view in Section 6.

2 Related Work

Interoperability of metadata is an important problem in many domains and harmonizing schemas from different sources has been recognized as a major challenge (Nilsson, 2010; Khoo and Hall, 2010; Nogueras-Iso et al., 2004). There are different approach to data integration. One approach consists on mapping data to one *monolithic* ontology that needs to be general enough to accommodate all the data categories from different sources. While this is appealing as it supports integrated querying of data, a single ontology cannot predict all aspects of metadata records, that all users may wish to record. In contrast, the linked data approach relies on multiple, standardized smaller and reusable vocabularies, each representing a subset of the data. In this line, some experts have recommended (Brooks and McCalla, 2006):

> "A larger set of ontologies sufficient for particular purposes should be used instead of a single highly constrained taxonomy of values."

In the context of linguistic data, different approaches have been pursued to collect metadata of resources. Large consortium-led projects and initiatives such as the CLARIN projects and META-NET have attempted to create metadata standards for representing linguistic data. Interoperability of the data stemming from these two repositories is however severely limited due to incompatibilities in their data models. META-SHARE favors a qualitative approach in which a relatively complex XML schema is provided to describe metadata of resources (Gavrilidou et al., 2012). At the same time, considerable effort has been devoted to ensuring data quality (Piperidis, 2012). In contrast, CLARIN does not provide a single schema, but a set of 'profiles' that are described in a schema language called the *CMDI Component Specification Language* (Broeder et al., 2012). Each institute describing resources using CMDI can instantiate the vocabulary to suit their particular needs. Similarly, an attempt has been made to catalogue language resources by assigning them a single unique identifier (Choukri et al., 2012).

Other more decentralized approaches are found in initiatives such as the LRE-Map (Calzolari et al., 2012) which provides a repository for researchers who want to submit the resources accompanying papers submitted to conferences. Most fields in LRE-Map consist of a text field with some prespecified options to select and a thorough analysis of the results has been conducted (Mariani et al., 2014).

Similarly, the *Open Linguistics Working Group* (Chiarcos et al., 2012) has been collecting language resources published as linked data in a

[2] http://www.ohchr.org/en/udhr/pages/introduction.aspx

Source	Records	RDF Triples	Triples per Record
META-SHARE	2,442	464,572	190.2
CLARIN VLO	144,570	3,381,736	23.4
Datahub.io	218	10,739	49.3
LRE-Map (LREC 2014)	682	10,650	15.6
LRE-Map (Non-open)	5,030	68,926	13.7
OLAC	217,765	2,613,183	12.0
ELRA Catalogue	1,066	22,580	21.2
LDC Catalogue	714	n/a	n/a

Table 1: The sizes of the resources in terms of number of metadata records and total data size

crowd-sourced repository at Datahub.io, in order to monitor the *Linguistic Linked Data cloud* and produce a diagram showing the status of these resources.

This clearly shows that the field is very fragmented, with different players using different approaches and most importantly different meta- and data models, thus impeding the discovery and integration of linguistic data.

3 Metadata collection and Schema Matching

In this section we describe the different methods applied to collect metadata from the different repositories:

- **META-SHARE:** For META-SHARE, a dump of the data was provided by the ILSP managing node of the META-NET project in XML format. We developed a custom script to convert this into the RDF data model, explicitly aligning data elements to the Dublin Core metadata vocabulary and add these as extra RDF triples to the root of the record. Frequently, these properties were deeply nested in the XML file and manual analysis was required to detect which instances truly applied to the entire metadata record.

- **CLARIN:** For CLARIN, we rely on the OAI-PMH (Sompel et al., 2004) framework to harvest data. The harvested OAI-PMH records comprise a header with basic information as well as a download link and a secondary XML description section that is structured according to the particular needs of the data provider. So far, we limit ourselves to collecting only those records that have Dublin Core properties.

- **LRE-Map:** For LRE-Map we used the available RDF/XML data dump[3], which contains submission information from the LREC 2014 conference, as well as data from other conferences, which is not freely available. In the RDF data, we gathered additional information about language resources, including the title of the paper describing the resource.

- **Datahub.io:** The data from Datahub.io was collected by means of the CKAN API[4]. As Datahub.io is a general-purpose catalogue we limited ourselves to extracting only those resources that were of relevance to linguistics. For this, we used an existing list of relevant categories and tags maintained by the Working Group on Open Linguistics (Chiarcos et al., 2012). The data model used by Datahub.io is also based on DCAT, so little adaptation of the data was required.

- **OLAC:** The Open Language Archives Community also relies on OAI-PMH to collect metadata and overlaps significantly with the CLARIN VLO. Unfortunately the data on this site is not openly licensed.

- **ELRA and LDC Catalogues:** These two organizations sell language resources and their catalogues are available online. The metadata records are not themselves openly licensed.

The total size in terms of records and triples (facts) as well as the average number of triples per repository are given in Table 1, where we can see significant differences in size and complexity of the resources. Note for the rest of this paper we will concern ourselves only with the openly licensed resources.

4 Metadata harmonization

As metadata has been obtained from different repositories, there are many incompatibilities between the values used in different resources. While some repositories ensure high-quality metadata in general, we also discovered inconsistencies in the use of values. For instance, while

[3] http://datahub.io/organization/institute-for-computational-linguistics-ilc-cnr

[4] http://datahub.io/api/3/ documented at http://docs.ckan.org/en/latest/api/index.html

META-SHARE recommends the use of ISO 639-3[5] tags for languages, a few data entries use English names for the language instead of the ISO code. We describe our approach to data value normalization below. In this initial harmonization phase we focused on the key questions of whether a resource is available, that is the given URL resolves, and whether the terms and conditions under which the resource can be used are specified. Further, we consider three key aspects that users need to know about resources to help them decide whether the resource matches their needs, namely: the type of the resource (corpus, lexical resource, etc.), intended use of the resource and languages covered. We note that many resources have multiple values for the same property (e.g., language), thus we allow multiple values at the record level, while still permitting more specific annotation deeper in the record.

4.1 Availability

In order to enable applications to (re)use language resources, we should find out if the resources described can still be accessed. For this we focused on the properties which were mapped to DCAT's 'access URL' property in the previous section. These 'access URLs' are intended to refer to HTML pages containing either download links or information on how to retrieve and use the resource. We augment the data with information about which links are valid and about the form of the content returned (e.g. HTML, XML, PDF, RDF/XML, etc.). Therefore, as we deal with heterogeneous sources and repositories, we analyzed access related characteristics and initially focused on answering two questions: *Is the language resource available and accessible on the Web and in what format?*.

To assess the current situation, we crawled and performed an analysis on a set of 119,290 URLs [6]. Our analysis showed that more than 95% of the URLs studied corresponded to accessible URLs (i.e., HTTP Response Code 200 OK), which indicates that in a high number of cases at least some information is provided to potential consumers of the resource.

Furthermore, our assessment showed that more than 66% of the accessible URLs corresponds to HTML pages, around 10% to RDF/XML documents, and other non-text formats sum up to almost 10% of the URLs analyzed (see Table 2). It is important to note that these results only describe what was returned by the service, and do not well reflect the actual format or availability of the data. For example, the high number of resources returning RDF/XML is mostly due to two CLARIN contributing institutes adopting RDF for their metadata.

Format	Resources	Percentage
HTML	67,419	66.2%
RDF/XML	9,940	9.8%
JPEG Image	6,599	6.5%
XML (application)	5,626	5.6%
Plain Text	4,251	4.2%
PDF	3,641	3.6%
XML (text)	3,212	3.2%
Zip Archive	801	0.8%
PNG Image	207	0.2%
gzip Archive	181	0.2%

Table 2: The distribution of the 10 most used formats within the analyzed sample of URLs. Note XML is associated with two MIME types.

4.2 Rights

Language resources are generally protected by copyright laws and they cannot be used against the terms expressed by the rights holders. These terms of use declare the actions that are authorized (e.g. derive, distribute) and the applicable conditions (e.g. attribution, the payment of a fee). They are an essential requirement for the reuse of a resource, but their automatic retrieval and processing is difficult because of the many forms they may adopt: rights information can appear either as a textual notice or as structured metadata, can consist of a mere reference to a well-known license (like an Open Data Commons or Creative Commons license), or it can point to an institution-specific document in a non-English language. These heterogeneous practices prevent the automated processing of licensing information.

Several challenges are posed for the harmonisation of the rights information: first, information is often not legally specified but instead vague statements such as 'freely available' are used; second, description of specific rights and conditions of each license requires complex modelling; and finally, due to the sensitivity of the information,

[5] `http://www-01.sil.org/iso639-3/`

[6] Due to crawling restrictions, only 60% of the URLs of the dataset were actually crawled

only high precision approaches should be applied.

From the RDF License dataset (Rodriguez-Doncel et al., 2014) we extracted the title, URI and abbreviation of the most commonly used licenses in different forms, and searched for exact matches normalizing for case, punctuation and whitespace. This introduced some errors due to dual-licensing schemes or misleading description were introduced. We manually evaluated all matching licenses and found 95.8% of the recognised strings were correctly matched. With this approach we could identify matching licenses for only 1% of the metadata entries. However, our observations suggest that this is due to the uninformative content for the license attribute. Furthermore, we note that more sophisticated methods have been shown to improve recall, but they do this at the cost of precision (Cabrio et al., 2014).

4.3 Usage

The language resource usage indicates the purpose and application for which the LR was created or which it has since be used. For META-SHARE we rely on the 83 values of the `useNLPSpecific` property and for LRE-Map we have a more limited list of 28 suggested values and many more user-provided free text entries, 3,985 in total (no other source contained this information). We manually mapped the 28 predefined values in LRE-Map to one of the 83 values predefined in META-SHARE. For the user-provided intended usage values, we developed a matching algorithm that identifies the corresponding META-SHARE intended use values. First we tokenized the expressions, then we stemmed the tokens using the Snowball stemmer (Porter, 2001), and we performed a string inclusion match, i.e. checking whether META-SHARE usages are included in the free text entries. For some entries we retrieved several matches (e.g. 'Document Classification, Text categorisation' matched both 'document classification' and 'text categorisation'), assuming that in the case of multiple matches the union of the intended usages was meant. With this algorithm we identified 66 matches on a random sample of 100 user-provided entries and they were all correct matches. From the remaining 34 unmatched entries, 16 were empty fields or non specific e.g. 'not applicable', 'various uses'. Other 16 entries were too general to be mapped to an intended use defined in the META-SHARE vocabulary e.g. 'testing', 'acquisition'. We had one false negative 'taggin pos'[sic] and one usage that is not yet in META-SHARE 'semantic system evaluation'. On this basis we had 98-99% accuracy on the results. Following the aforementioned algorithm we identified 65% matches on the entire set of user-entries. We further investigated the remaining 35% non-matches and we identified further intended use values that are not yet in META-SHARE vocabulary, e.g. 'entity linking', 'corpus creation', which we will suggest as extensions of the META-SHARE vocabulary.

4.4 Language

To clean the names of languages contained in metadata records, we aligned to the ISO 639-3 standard. First we extracted all the language labels from our records and obtained a total of 833 distinct language labels. Next we leveraged two resources to map these noisy language labels to standard ISO codes: (i) the official SIL database[7], which contains all the standard ISO codes and their *English* names, and (ii) BabelNet[8] (Navigli and Ponzetto, 2012), a large multilingual lexico-semantic resource containing, among others, translations and synonyms of various language names along with their ISO codes.

To perform the mapping in an automatic manner, we compared each of the 833 noisy language labels against the language labels contained in SIL and BabelNet using two string similarity algorithms: the *Dice coefficient* string similarity algorithm and the *Levenshtein* distance string metric.

Table 3 reports an excerpt of the results showcasing in the first row a match for all cases, in the second a match for BabelNet but not for SIL, and in the third a mismatch for all. Furthermore, the final row reports a mismatch from Levenshtein, where 'Turkish, Crimean' is matched instead.

In order to measure the accuracy of each approach we tested the mapping algorithms against a manually annotated dataset containing 100 language labels and ISO codes. In Table 4, we present the accuracy of our methods based on the number of labels correctly identified ("label accuracy") and the accuracy weighted for the number of metadata records with that label ("instance accuracy"). The best results are obtained using BabelNet as the source of language labels. Babel-

[7] `http://www-01.sil.org/iso639-3/download.asp`

[8] `http://babelnet.org/`

Input	Expected output	BabelNet output		SIL output	
		dice	*leven*	*dice*	*leven*
Kurdish	kur	kur	kur	kur	kur
rank – distance		1	0	1	0
label		Kurdish	Kurdish	kurdish	Kurdish
Bokmål	nob	nob	nob	bok*	bdt*
rank – distance		1	0	0.57	3
label		bokmål	Bokmål	bok	Bokoto
Ñahñú (Otomí)	oto	omq*	otm*	ttf*	las*
rank – distance		0.38	8	0.35	7
label		Otomí Mangue	Eastern Otomí	tuotomb	lama (togo)
Turkish (Türkçe)	tur	tur	tur	tur	crh*
rank – distance		0.7	6	0.7	7
label		Turkish	Türkiye Türkçesi	turkish	Turkish, Crimean

Table 3: Excerpt output of language mapping. * indicates mismatches.

Resource	Label Accuracy	Instance Accuracy
SIL *dice coefficient*	81%	99.50%
SIL *levenshtein*	72%	99.42%
BabelNet *dice coefficient*	**91%**	99.87%
BabelNet *levenshtein*	**89%**	99.85%
SIL + BabelNet		
dice coefficient	**91%**	99.87%
levenshtein	**89%**	99.85%

Table 4: Accuracy of language mappings

Net is more accurate in matching language labels, largely because it contains translations, synonyms and obsolete spellings of most, even rare or dialectal, languages. SIL on the other hand only contains the English representation of each ISO code, failing to induce certain mappings. Furthermore, the Dice coefficient string similarity algorithm yields more accurate results compared to the Levenshtein distance metric. We hypothesize that this is mainly due to the fact that the Dice coefficient is more lenient compared to the Levensthein metric as it is insensitive to the order of words. For instance, using Dice coefficient, the input label 'Quechua de Cotahuasi (Arequipa)' matches 'Cotahuasi Quechua' correctly. With the Levenshtein algorithm, however, using the same input as earlier, the label 'Quechua cajamarquino' is mistakenly matched instead.

Overall, combining BabelNet and SIL yields the same normalization accuracy as BabelNet alone.

Resource	Duplicate Titles	Duplicate URLs
CLARIN (same contributing institute)	50,589	20
Datahub.io	0	55
META-SHARE	63	967

Table 5: The number of intra-repository duplicate labels and URLs for resources

Nonetheless, we can observe a slight decrease in the average distance returned by the Levensthein algorithm. The addition of a multilingual semantic database, such as BabelNet, positively affects the ability to match obsolete names in different languages.

4.5 Type

The type property is used primarily to describe the kind of resource being described. For META-SHARE, we can rely on the structure of resources to extract one of four primary resource types, namely, 'Corpus', 'Lexical Conceptual Resource', 'Lexical Description' and 'Tool Service'. However, for the other sources considered in this paper the type field permits free text input. In order to enable users to query resources by type we ran the Babelfy entity linking algorithm (Moro et al., 2014) to identify entities in the string and then manually selected elements from this list of entities that described the kind of resource, such as 'corpus'. In this way we extracted, 143 categories for language resources while still ensuring that syntactic variations were accounted for. The top 10 categories extracted in this way were: 'Sound', 'Corpus', 'Lexicon', 'Tool' (software), 'Instrumental Music'[9], 'Service', 'Ontology', 'Evaluation', 'Terminology' and 'Translation software'.

5 Duplicate detection

As we are collecting and indexing metadata records from different repositories, it is possible to find duplicates, that is records that describe the same actual resource. In fact, duplicate entries did not only occur across repositories (we dub these *inter-repository duplicates*) but also within the same resource (referred to as *intra-repository duplicates*). We expand the definition of inter-repository by noting that CLARIN is sourced from a number of different contribut-

[9]These resources are in fact recordings of singing in under-resourced languages

ing institutes and there are duplicates between institutes, thus we consider links between records of different CLARIN institutes as *inter-repository*. Similarly, there has been no attempt to manage duplicates in LRE-Map and so we handle all links between LRE-Map records as *inter-repository*.

In order to detect duplicates, we rely on two properties that should be unique across entries, that is the title and the 'access URL'. In Table 5 we show the number of records with duplicate titles or URLs. Manual inspection of these duplicates yielded the following observations:

META-SHARE META-SHARE contains a number of duplicate titles. However, these title duplicates seem to be errors in the export and can thus be easily corrected.

CLARIN Many resources in CLARIN are described across many records. For example, in CLARIN there may be one different metadata record for each chapter of a book or recording within an audio or television collection, or in at least one case ("The Universal Declaration of Human Rights") a record exists for each language the resource is available in. Thus, we decided to merge the entries which share the same title and same contributing institute in CLARIN.

Datahub.io The creation method of DataHub prevents the creation of different entries with the same title, so duplicate titles do not occur in the data. However, we found a number of entries having the same download URL. This is due to the fact that different resources share SPARQL endpoints or download pages, but the records did not describe the same resource and so we did not merge these resources.

Table 6 shows the number of resources with the same title (Duplicate Titles), same URL (Duplicate URLs) as well as same title **and** same URL within and across repositories. We apply the following strategy in handling duplicates:

Intra-repository duplicates As intra-repository duplicates are mostly either system errors or series of closely related resources, we simply merge the corresponding metadata entries. If a property is one-to-one we take only the first value.

Duplication	Correct	Unclear	Incorrect
Titles	86	6	8
URLs	95	2	3
Both	99	1	0

Table 7: Precision of matching strategies from a sample of 100

Property	Record Count (As percentage of all records)	Triples
Access URL	91,615 (91.6%)	191,006
Language	50,781 (50.7%)	98,267
Type	15,241 (15.2%)	17,894
Rights	3,080 (3.0%)	8915
Usage	3,397 (3.4%)	4,530

Table 8: Number of records and facts harmonized by our methods

Inter-repository duplicates Inter-repository duplicates represent multiple records of the same underlying resource, they are linked to one another by the 'close match' property.

Note we do not remove duplicates from the dataset we either combine them into a more structured record or mark them as deprecated.

We evaluate the precision of this approach on a sample of 100 inter-repository entries identified as duplicates according to the above mentioned approach. We manually classify the matches into *correct*, *incorrect* as well as *unclear*, if there was insufficient information to make a decision, the resources overlapped or were different versions of each other. Table 7 shows these results. We see that with 99% precision the method identifying duplicates if both title and URL match yields the best results. While the recall is difficult to assess, an analysis of the data quickly reveals that there are many duplicates not detected using this method. For example, for the Stanford Parser (De Marneffe et al., 2006), we find metadata records with all of the following titles: "Stanford Parser", "Stanford Dependency Parser", "Stanford Lexicalized Parser", "Stanford's NLP Parser", "The Stanford Parser", "The Stanford Parser: A Lexicalized Parser".

6 Discussion

The rapid developments of natural language processing technologies in the last few years has resulted in a very large number of language resources being created and made available on the

Resource	Resource	Duplicate Titles	Duplicate URLs	Both
CLARIN	CLARIN (other contributing institute)	1,202	2,884	0
CLARIN	Datahub.io	1	0	0
CLARIN	LRE-Map	72	64	0
CLARIN	META-SHARE	1,204	1,228	28
Datahub.io	LRE-Map	59	5	0
Datahub.io	META-SHARE	3	0	0
LRE-Map	LRE-Map	763	454	359
LRE-Map	META-SHARE	91	51	0
All	All	3,395	4,686	387

Table 6: Number of duplicate inter-repository records by type

web. In order to enable these resources to be reused appropriately it is necessary to properly document resources and make this available as structured, queriable metadata on the Web. Current approaches to metadata collection are either *curatorial*, where dedicated workers maintain metadata of high quality, such as the approach employed by META-SHARE. This approach ensures metadata quality but is very expensive and as such it is unlikely that it will be able to handle the vast number of resources published every year. In contrast, *crowd-sourced* resources rely primarily on self-reporting of metadata, and this approach has a high recall but is very error-prone and this unreliability can be plainly seen in resources such as LRE-Map. In this paper, we have aimed to break this dichotomy by aggregating resources from both curated and crowd-sourced resources, and applied natural language processing techniques to provide a basic level of compliance among these metadata records, and have achieved this for a large number of records as summarized in table 8. In this sense we have considered a small set of properties that we regard as essential for the description and discovery of relevant language resource, that is: resource type, language, intended use, and licensing conditions. For the language property we have shown that it can be harmonized across repositories with high accuracy by mapping values to a controlled vocabulary list, although the data indicated that there were still many languages which were not covered in the ISO lists. For the type, rights and usage properties, whose content is not as limited, it is harder to harmonize but we were still able to show that in many cases these results can be connected to known lists of values. This is important as it would allow for easier queries of the resource.

Besides harmonizing values of data, we see two further key aspects to ensure quality of the metadata. First, broken links should be avoided as they are indicators of low curation and low quality. Thus, we automatically detect such broken URLs and remove them from the dataset. A second crucial issue is the removal of duplicates, which are also a sign of low quality.

We have investigated different strategies for detecting duplicates. We observed that the case in which two metadata records have been provided to different repositories is common. When integrating data from different repositories, these entries become duplicated. In other cases, particularly in CLARIN, different metadata records are created for parts of a resource. Genuine duplication likely affects about 7% of records, underlining the value of collecting resources from multiple sources. We further note that it is important to take a high precision approach to deduplication as the merging of non-duplicate resources can hide resources entirely from the query. Thus, we have proposed high-precision methods for detecting such duplicates.

Finally, we note that the data resulting from this process is available under the Creative Commons Attribution Non-Commercial ShareALike License and the data can be queried through a portal, which is available at **URL anonymized**. Furthermore, all code described in this paper is accessible from a popular open source repository.[10]

7 Conclusion

We have studied the task of harmonizing records of language resources that are heterogeneous on several levels and have shown that the applica-

[10]To remain anonymous we cannot include URLs for these resources at this point

tion of NLP techniques allows to provide common metadata that will better enable users to find language resources for their specific applications. We note that this work is still on-going and should be improved in not only the accuracy and coverage of harmonization, but also in the number of properties that are harmonized (authorship and subject topic are planned). We hope that this new approach to handling language resource metadata will better enable users to find language resources and assist in the creation of new domains of study in computational linguistics.

Acknowledgments

LingHub was made possible due to significant help from a large number of people, in particular we would like to thank the following people: Benjamin Siemoneit (Bielefeld University), Tiziano Flati (University of Rome, La Sapienza), Martin Brümmer (University of Leipzig), Sebastian Hellmann (University of Leipzig), Bettina Klimek (University of Leipzig), Penny Labropolou (IEA-ILSP), Juli Bakagianni (IEA-ILSP), Stelios Piperidis (IEA-ILSP), Nicoletta Calzolari (ILC-CNR), Riccardo del Gratta (ILC-CNR), Marta Villegas (Pompeu Fabra), Núria Bel (Pompeu Fabra), Asunción Gómez-Pérez (Universidad Politécnica de Madrid) and Christian Chiarcos (Goethe-University Frankfurt).

This work was funded by the LIDER ("Linked Data as an enabler of cross-media and multilingual content analytics for enterprises across Europe"), an FP7 project refererence number 610782 in the topic ICT-2013.4.1: Content analytics and language technologies.

References

Daan Broeder, Marc Kemps-Snijders, Dieter Van Uytvanck, Menzo Windhouwer, Peter Withers, Peter Wittenburg, and Claus Zinn. 2010. A data category registry-and component-based metadata framework. In *Proceedings of the 7th International Conference on Language Resources and Evaluation*, pages 43–47.

Daan Broeder, Menzo Windhouwer, Dieter Van Uytvanck, Twan Goosen, and Thorsten Trippel. 2012. CMDI: a component metadata infrastructure. In *Describing LRs with metadata: towards flexibility and interoperability in the documentation of LR workshop programme*, page 1.

Christopher Brooks and Gord McCalla. 2006. Towards flexible learning object metadata. *Continuing Engineering Education and Lifelong Learning*, 16(1/2):50–63.

Elena Cabrio, Alessio Palmero Aprosio, and Serena Villata. 2014. These are your rights: A natural language processing approach to automated RDF licenses generation. In *The Semantic Web: Trends and Challenges*, pages 255–269. Springer.

Nicoletta Calzolari, Riccardo Del Gratta, Gil Francopoulo, Joseph Mariani, Francesco Rubino, Irene Russo, and Claudia Soria. 2012. The LRE Map. Harmonising community descriptions of resources. In *Proceedings of the 8th International Conference on Language Resources and Evaluation*, pages 1084–1089.

Christian Chiarcos, Sebastian Hellmann, and Sebastian Nordhoff. 2012. The Open Linguistics Working Group of the Open Knowledge Foundation. In *Linked Data in Linguistics*, pages 153–160. Springer.

Khalid Choukri, Victoria Arranz, Olivier Hamon, and Jungyeul Park. 2012. Using the international standard language resource number: Practical and technical aspects. In *Proceedings of the 8th International Conference on Language Resources and Evaluation*, pages 50–54.

Marie-Catherine De Marneffe, Bill MacCartney, Christopher D Manning, et al. 2006. Generating typed dependency parses from phrase structure parses. In *Proceedings of LREC*, volume 6, pages 449–454.

Christian Federmann, Ioanna Giannopoulou, Christian Girardi, Olivier Hamon, Dimitris Mavroeidis, Salvatore Minutoli, and Marc Schröder. 2012. META-SHARE v2: An open network of repositories for language resources including data and tools. In *Proceedings of the 8th International Conference on Language Resources and Evaluation*, pages 3300–3303.

Maria Gavrilidou, Penny Labropoulou, Elina Desipri, Stelios Piperidis, Harris Papageorgiou, Monica Monachini, Francesca Frontini, Thierry Declerck, Gil Francopoulo, Victoria Arranz, et al. 2012. The META-SHARE metadata schema for the description of language resources. In *Proceedings of the 8th International Conference on Language Resources and Evaluation*, pages 1090–1097.

Michael Khoo and Catherine Hall. 2010. Merging metadata: a sociotechnical study of crosswalking and interoperability. In *Proceedings of the 10th annual joint conference on Digital libraries*, pages 361–364. ACM.

Joseph Mariani, Christopher Cieri, Gil Francopoulou, Patrick Paroubek, and Marine Delaborde. 2014. Facing the identification problem in language-related scientific data analysis. In *Proceedings of the 9th International Conference on Language Resources and Evaluation*, pages 2199–2205.

Andrea Moro, Alessandro Raganato, and Roberto Navigli. 2014. Entity linking meets word sense disambiguation: a unified approach. *Transactions of the Association for Computational Linguistics (TACL)*, 2:231–244.

Roberto Navigli and Simone Paolo Ponzetto. 2012. BabelNet: The automatic construction, evaluation and application of a wide-coverage multilingual semantic network. *Artificial Intelligence*, 193:217–250.

Mikael Nilsson. 2010. *From interoperability to harmonization in metadata standardization*. Ph.D. thesis, Royal Institute of Technology.

Javier Nogueras-Iso, F Javier Zarazaga-Soria, Javier Lacasta, Rubén Béjar, and Pedro R Muro-Medrano. 2004. Metadata standard interoperability: application in the geographic information domain. *Computers, environment and urban systems*, 28(6):611–634.

Stelios Piperidis. 2012. The META-SHARE language resources sharing infrastructure: Principles, challenges, solutions. In *Proceedings of the 8th International Conference on Language Resources and Evaluation*, pages 36–42.

Martin F Porter. 2001. Snowball: A language for stemming algorithms.

Victor Rodriguez-Doncel, Serena Villata, and Asuncion Gomez-Perez. 2014. A dataset of RDF licenses. In Rinke Hoekstra, editor, *Proceedings of the 27th International Conference on Legal Knowledge and Information System*, pages 187–189.

Gary Simons and Steven Bird. 2003. The open language archives community: An infrastructure for distributed archiving of language resources. *Literary and Linguistic Computing*, 18(2):117–128.

Herbert van de Sompel, Michael L Nelson, Carl Lagoze, and Simeon Warner. 2004. Resource harvesting within the OAI-PMH framework. *D-Lib Magazine*, 10(12).

Digital Representation of Rights for Language Resources

Victor Rodriguez-Doncel
Ontology Engineering Group
Universidad Politécnica de Madrid
vrodriguez@delicias.dia.upm.es

Penny Labropoulou
Institute for Language and Speech Processing
Athena RC - Athens
penny@ilsp.athena-innovation.gr

Abstract

Language resources are very often valuable assets which are offered to the public under the terms of licenses that determine which uses are allowed and under which circumstances. These licenses have been typically published as natural language texts whose specific contents cannot be easily processed by a computer. This paper proposes a structured representation for the most commonly used licenses for language resources, reusing existing vocabularies and extending the Open Digital Rights Language core model. Examples and guidelines to use the 'Rights Information for Language Resources' vocabulary are given.

1 Introduction

Computational Linguistics started some 50 years ago studying natural language from a computational perspective. The need for Language Resources (LRs), such as lexica, thesauri, terminologies and corpora, was soon appreciated. At first, LRs producers created them mainly for their own use; however it was soon clear that LRs with a minimum size and quality, as those required for the advancement of Computational Linguistics and related disciplines could only live in a sharing paradigm, with LRs being created, distributed, used, re-used, extended and enriched in a shared environment.

LRs were offered to other users, following various distribution models: some LR producers publishing and promoting their resources themselves, either through their institutional sites or through sites dedicated to particular LRs, other producers forming alliances together with other interested parties in order to distribute but also to create new resources (e.g. LDC[1]) or passing on the distribution of their resources to dedicated agencies (e.g. ELRA/ELDA[2], TST-Centrale[3]) etc. The majority of LRs were offered for research and educational purposes, at no cost or for a minimal fee, especially when produced by public funding. The situation, however, changed mainly as the development of Language Technology led to the appearance of profitable business, which also led to the realization that LRs could also be a source of profit. As a consequence, some of the LR publishers have opted to market their LRs (or the rights thereof), thus making licensing an indispensable aspect in the distribution of LRs.

When discussing about licensing of LRs, two are the main dimensions that need to be taken into account: (a) the license itself, either in the form of a proper legal document, or some loosely expressed legal notice, (b) the clear indication of the licensing terms on the LR, in the form of free text or conventional metadata.

One of the priorities set by the FLARENET Strategic Research Agenda (Soria et al., 2014) is the availability of LRs "within an adequate IPR[4] and legal framework". The recommendations include the elaboration of "specific, simple and *harmonised licensing solutions* for data resources", taking into account licensing schemes already in use and simplifying them through broad-based solutions for both R & D and industry, and the adoption of *electronic licensing* and adaptation of current distribution models to new media (web, mobile devices etc.).

The digital formulation of rights and the standardisation of the licensing vocabulary have a number of advantages such as:

- improvement of the understanding of the li-

[1] https://www.ldc.upenn.edu/
[2] http://www.elra.info/en/
[3] http://tst-centrale.org/nl/home
[4] IPR: Intellectual Property Rights

Proceedings of the 4th Workshop on Linked Data in Linguistics (LDL-2015), pages 49–58,
Beijing, China, July 31, 2015.

censing terms by human users: although licenses are natural language texts, the legal jargon is quite complicated and not easily understood by newcomers. A harmonised vocabulary for licensing terms favours universal understanding of their precise meaning; moreover, the non-flat structure of digital rights information also favours the understanding of the different modalities (e.g. 'free if used for research', but 'non-free if used for commercial purposes')

- processing of the licensing terms by machines; this is extremely important in a reuse scenario of LRs, whereby they can be automatically processed by web services, combined with other LRs, extended and enriched: only LRs that allow such actions should be involved in these activities; and this can only be asserted if rights are expressed in a way understood by machines
- enhancement of the discovery of LRs that allow/forbid particular conditions of use through filtered browsing of LR catalogs based on criteria such as "license", "conditions of use" and "access rights"
- better management of the LRs by publishers, who have a clearer account on which rights have been granted to which resources.

Among the digital structures for representing the rights information, RDF is the one which best favours interoperability. The emergence of the Linked Data paradigm as a manner of publishing LRs on the web urged the publication of licensing information as Linked Data as well. This paper describes a language for expressing rights information for LRs as RDF, starting by the groundings in Section 2 (reviewing the existent practice and the requirements collected), continuing with the ontology in Section 3 and finalizing with examples and conclusions in Section 4 and 5 respectively.

2 Motivation for a common model

2.1 Rights information in LR repositories

LRs are in general considered intellectual property works, and as such they are protected by copyright laws: they should not be used in violation of the terms set by the rights holders. The terms of use declare the actions that are authorized (e.g. whether they allow derivation, redistribution) and the applicable conditions (e.g. whether they require attribution, payment of a fee). The terms are included in the documentation of most LRs, but their automatic retrieval and processing is difficult because of the many forms they adopt: rights information may appear either as a textual notice or as structured metadata elements, it may consist of a mere reference to a well-known license (like an Open Data Commons or Creative Commons license), or it may point to a license drafted in a non-English language to be used solely for the specific resource. These heterogeneous practices prevent the automated processing of rights information.

Recently, we witness the proliferation of repositories collecting LRs and their metadata descriptions from various communities and sources according to different harvesting methodologies, and publishing them into homogeneous catalogs. The most relevant initiatives for our discussion are: META-SHARE[5] (Piperidis, 2012), CLARIN[6], LRE-Map[7] (Calzolari et al., 2012), OLAC[8] (Simons and Bird, 2003) and Datahub.io[9].

Taking a closer look at the rights metadata present in these catalogs, we see the following tendencies:

- catalogs where the rights information is loosely represented as a free text metadata element: this is mainly the case for portals harvesting from various sources, such as OLAC, the LRE Map and the CLARIN Virtual Language Observatory (VLO[10]); the reason for this is the fact that the sources do not oblige the depositors to document the access rights and/or allow them to use natural language statements for that (e.g. "free for research", "available at resource owner's site", "Public domain resource" etc.); this is also due to the fact that they include resources whose licenses are not available over the internet (e.g. resources from older times, when licenses were not standardised and providers asked legal experts to draft specific contracts for each resource, which were made available only to interested parties upon request); for the LRE Map, this practice has been dictated by the

[5] http://www.meta-share.eu
[6] http://www.clarin.eu
[7] http://www.resourcebook.eu
[8] http://www.language-archives.org/
[9] http://www.datahub.io
[10] http://catalog.clarin.eu/vlo

fact that the metadata are submitted by authors of papers in conferences (e.g. LREC) describing the resources connected to their publication, which may still be under construction and/or not yet be available for distribution with specific licenses, so they simply indicate their intentions;

- catalogs where the rigths information is represented with a controlled vocabulary of values referring to standard licenses; this is the case of META-SHARE and partly Datahub and the CLARIN network repositories; in the case of Datahub, when registering a new dataset, providers can choose a license from a list, but also licensing information can be found in the VoID description of the dataset or even within the dataset itself. In META-SHARE, the provider is also forced to select for the license element among a controlled list of values corresponding to recommended standard licenses[11]; this element (as described in the following section) is part of a more complicated set of metadata elements describing the distribution conditions of the LR. In the case of CLARIN, there is a set of recommended licenses that LR providers are asked to use when depositing their resources in the repositories of the infrastructure, but legacy data can of course come with their own licenses; to help users understand the access rights, licenses are classified to one of three categories: those that can be publicly distributed (PUB), those permitting only academic use, i.e. use for research and educational purposes and which require user authentication, i.e. that users' identity is known (ACA) and those which impose additional restrictions or whose use requires additional consent from the rightsholder (RES); the use of easy-to-understand icons and symbols (e.g. a money icon for resources distributed with-a-fee) is recommended (Oksanen and Lindn, 2011).

- faceted browsing with the criterion of access rights/ license is a feature integrated in most of these catalogs but it is actually useful mostly when the set of values is limited to a manageable number of values that users can browse through; in addition, META-SHARE allows faceted browsing with a filter for conditions of use (e.g. whether the license allows commercial use, derivatives etc.)

[11] http://www.meta-net.eu/meta-share/licenses

The most recent initiative in this line is the Linghub portal[12], supported by the European LIDER project, which collects metadata from some of the repositories mentioned before (META-SHARE, CLARIN, Datahub.io and LRE Map) and publishes the records as Linked Data. All licensing information present in the original metadata records is harvested and collected together in the element "rights", bringing together license names, urls, free text statements etc. The work presented in this paper is related to this effort and the need for a common licensing metadata framework (McCrae et al., 2015).

2.2 Rights information in the META-SHARE model

The META-SHARE (MS) metadata schema constitutes an essential ingredient of the META-SHARE infrastructure, which is an open, integrated, secure and interoperable exchange infrastructure where LRs are documented, uploaded, stored, catalogued, announced, downloaded, exchanged and discussed, aiming to support reuse of LRs (Piperidis, 2012). The MS schema is a complex but rich model and, most important for our work, provides extensive support for the detailed representation of licensing information, making a remarkable effort that in some regards goes beyond of what has been described by license-specialized models. In consequence, the MS model has been taken as a basis for the rest of this work.

The original META-SHARE metadata model (Gavrilidou et al., 2012) [13] has been implemented as an XML Schema[14]. The META-SHARE schema encodes information about the whole life-cycle of the LR from production to usage. The central entity of the schema is the LR per se, which encompasses both datasets and technologies used for their processing. In addition to the

[12] http://linghub.lider-project.eu/

[13] Documentation and User Manual of the META-SHARE Metadata Model, found at http://www.meta-net.eu/meta-share/META-SHARE\%20\%20documentationUserManual.pdf

[14] Schemas can be found at github https://github.com/metashare/META-SHARE/tree/master/misc/schema/v3.0

central entity, other entities are also documented in the schema; these are reference *documents* related to the LR (papers, reports, manuals etc.), *persons/organizations* involved in its creation and use (creators, distributors etc.), related *projects* and activities (funding projects, activities of usage etc.) and accompanying *licenses*, all described with metadata taken as far as possible from relevant schemas and guidelines (e.g. BibTex for bibliographical references). The five root entities are represented as boxes in Figure 1. The META-SHARE schema proposes a set of elements to encode specific descriptive features of each of these entities and relations holding between them, taking as a starting point the LR. Following the CMDI approach (Broeder et al., 2012), these elements are grouped together into "components". The core of the schema is the *resourceInfo* component, which subsumes

- administrative components relevant to all LRs, e.g. *identificationInfo* (name, description and identifiers), *usageInfo* (information about the intended and actual use of the LR);
- components specific to the relevant resource and media type combinations, e.g. text or audio parts of corpora, lexical/conceptual resources etc., such as language, formats, classification etc.

The META-SHARE schema recognises obligatory elements (minimal version) and recommended and optional elements (maximal version).

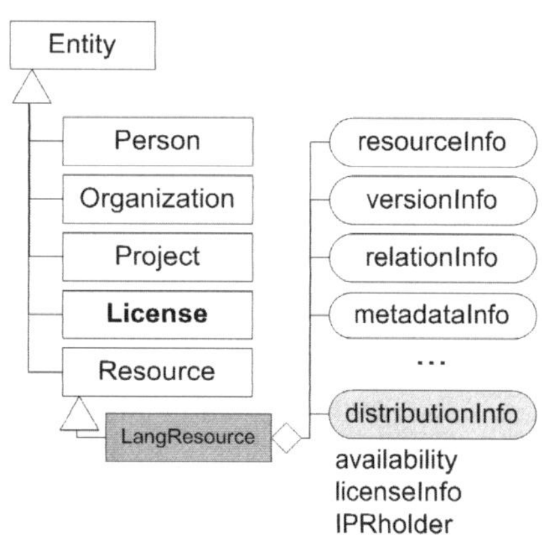

Figure 1: Main entities in the MS model

For our discussion, the most relevant component is the *distributionInfo* which brings together all information related to licensing and IPR issues, e.g. the IPR holder(s), the distribution rights holder(s), availability status (i.e. whether the LR is available for access, with or without restrictions); the embedded *licenseInfo* component encodes all information related to the licensing terms, e.g. the license short name and specific terms and conditions, the medium with which the LR can be accessed (i.e. whether it cam be downloaded or used via an i/f etc.). Each resource may be linked to one or more *licenseInfo* components, in case the same resource is made available under different formats and/or licensing conditions (e.g. for free for non-commercial purposes vs. at a price for commercial purposes, downloadable for commercial users vs. accessible through interface for academic users).

In the framework of the LD4LT group, the META-SHARE model has been the base for the development of an ontology in OWL; the MS/OWL ontology has been based on the on the ontology developed by Villegas et al. (Villegas et al., 2014) (covering part of the original schema) and extended to the complete schema (in order to cover all relevant LRs) (McCrae et al., 2015). The transformation from the XSD schema to the OWL ontology involved the transformation of components to classes and that of elements to properties[15].

3 The Rights Information for Language Resources Ontology

In the course of this activity, the original module of licensing and rights information has been re-structured (in order to better accommodate RDF modelling considerations) and enhanced with RELs, capable of describing rights information in a generally understood manner. RELs also provide a hierarchical organization for the rights information whose structure more naturally depicts dual licenses, nested permissions and the relationship between conditions and rights. In addition, some other vocabularies like CreativeCommons'[16] or the price specification with GoodRelations have been considered.

The licensing and rights module as perceived in the model has also been released as a separate ontology ("Rights Information for Language Resources" ontology) at:

[15] This is an simplified description of the actual transformation process; for more on this, see (McCrae et al., 2015)

[16] `http://creativecommons.org/ns#`

http://purl.org/NET/ms-rights

The rights ontology builds upon the META-SHARE schema for the LanguageResource and the Distribution classes and for the License class integrates elements of the ODRL model. In fact, the ontology revolves around three entities/-classes:

- the *Language Resource*, perceived in the same way as in the original MS model;
- the *Distribution*, which comes from the original *distributionInfo* component but is remodeled and adapted to the concept of the *dcat:Distribution*[17] class; thus, it now represents an accessible form of an LR, which for instance can be available through different delivery channels (e.g. as a downloadable file, on a CD-ROM or accessible via an interface), in different forms (e.g. as a csv or txt file), through different distributors and with different licensing terms;
- the License, coming from the *licenseInfo* component.

The elements included in the *distributionInfo* and *licenseInfo* components have been transformed to OWL object and datatype properties, while a careful study has been made in order to attach them to the appropriate classes. For instance, the *iprHolder* which was included in the *distributionInfo* component has been attached to the *Language Resource* class, given that this is a property that remains the same irrespective of the different forms of access an LR may take; the *distributionRightsHolder*, however, may differ for different forms and is thus attached to the *Distribution* class. Similarly, there has been a careful separation of the elements included in the *licenseInfo* between properties attached to the license and those moved to the *Distribution* class. Here, the main consideration was to detach the License class from Language resources, in an effort to generalize over them and standardize their representation as far as possible. By attaching, for instance, the exact sum to be paid for the acquisition of an LR to the Distribution class while the information that a payment is due on the license class, we can re-use the same license representation for all LRs distributed under this condition.

We have also introduced additional properties (e.g. *licenseCategory*, *licenseName* and *licenseURL*) and individuals (*languageEngineeringResearch* for the *ConditionsOfUse*).

Licenses represented with the Rights Information for Language Resources ontology permit a dual representation of the information: preserving the META-SHARE elements and structure and/or adhering to the ODRL schema. Both are compatible and satisfy different requirements. Redundancy is the preferred option, but expressing rights information in either manner is acceptable. This section describes both alternatives, introducing first the ODRL-style and then the schema inherited from META-SHARE.

3.1 Rights Expressions in ODRL

ODRL 2.1[18] is a policy and rights expression language suitable to represent the licensing terms of the language resources. ODRL specifies both an abstract core model and a common vocabulary, which can be extended for the particular domains ODRL is applied to. There have been ODRL profiles for representing contents' rights in mobile devices (OMA DRM), for the news industry (RightsML by IPTC), for the eBook (ONIX) and for general Creative Commons licenses, but no specific terms exist for the language resources domain. ODRL 2.0 can be serialized in XML, JSON and RDF. The latter serialization is based on the ODRL 2.1 Ontology (McRoberts and Rodriguez-Doncel (eds.), 2015).

The main entities in the ODRL Core Model[19] are presented in Figure 2. An ODRL *policy* is a set of *rules*, which can be *permissions*, *prohibitions* or *duties*. Permissions allow executing certain *actions* over an *asset*, provided that certain *constraints* are respected. An *assignee* can be specified for the action to be executed by.

The example of ODRL expression in Figure 3, serialized as RDF describes a language resource as being reproducible (downloaded, copied) but not derivable nor commercializable[20]. The absence of assignee is understood as 'applicable to anybody'.

[17] The prefix *dcat* stands for Data Catalog Vocabulary. DCAT is a W3C Recommendation http://www.w3.org/TR/vocab-dcat/

[18] https://www.w3.org/community/odrl/

[19] http://www.w3.org/community/odrl/model/2/

[20] The prefix *odrl* points to http://www.w3.org/ns/odrl/2/

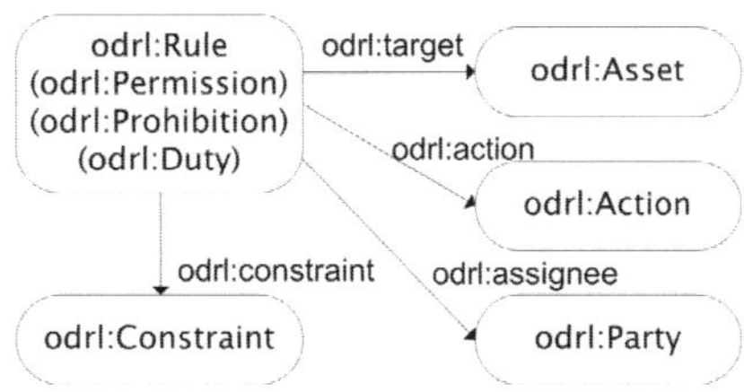

Figure 2: Main entities in the ODRL model

```
:example0
 a odrl:Set;
 odrl:permission [
   odrl:target :langResource ;
   odrl:action odrl:reproduce
 ] ;
 odrl:prohibition [
   odrl:target :langResource ;
   odrl:action odrl:derive,
     odrl:commercialize
 ] .
```

Figure 3: Simple example of ODRL policy

3.2 Rights expression within the META-SHARE structure

The ODRL model satisfies most of the concepts that are required for the licensing of LRs. Some adjustments have been required mainly to separate general conditions from the specifics that can instantiate them: for instance, payment is a general term of use but the exact amount to be paid for each LR may differ and vary depending on a number of other parameters (e.g. no fee for non-commercial use, X euros for commercial use, X euros but with a discount for a specific group of users etc.); by keeping the payment as a general condition in the RDF representation of the license and putting the amount to be paid on the LR, we can have the same standard license used for a large number of LRs. Consequently, the semantics of the ODRL model have been slightly altered for the Rights Information for Language Resources: *missing attributes in the policy can be found as attributes of the licensed asset.* Besides the vocabulary additions over the ODRL Common Vocabulary, which are foreseen by the specification, this is the only divergence that was made from the ODRL language.

The primary META-SHARE metadata schema presents conditions and rights in a flat structure. While this information is expressed in ODRL within the rules, having it directly accessible improves readability by simple processors. Hence,

```
:langResource a ms:languageResource .
:langResource ms:distribution :distrib1 .
:distrib1 dct:license :lic1 .
:lic1 ms:conditionsOfUse ms:noRedistri-
  bution, ms:nonCommercialUse .
```

Figure 5: Example equivalent to 3 using the MS structure

as a second design decision, *rights and conditions can be redundantly given as attributes of the policy or within the rule structure.*

The licensing information of a language resource can be entirely described with the MS/OWL ontology. In Figure 4, key classes are represented with orange ovals and minor classes with gray ovals. Class individuals are rectangles next to a class they are instances of. Properties are represented with arrows. For our regards, the four key elements in the META-SHARE structure are: a 'language resource' is published as a 'distribution', which may have attached a 'license'. 'Licenses' can have 'conditions of use'. The language resource can have different levels of availability (restricted, unrestricted, upon negotiation etc.). The distribution has a specific access medium and it can be granted to users of different nature (academic users, commercial users, etc. or combinations thereof). Licensors and distribution rights holders can also be expressed at the distribution level.

The License can belong to a License Category (ACA, RES, PUB) and it may contain different conditions of use –the fine grain but flat description of the license.

4 Examples of license

In the most simple setting, the metadata records describing a language resource may point to an RDF document with the license description. The RDF License dataset (Rodriguez-Doncel et al., 2014) contains a set of well-known licenses and licenses recommended by META-SHARE[21] which have been already written using the elements of the ontology.

To facilitate end users, we identified commonly used licenses in the LR domain from the values used for LRs distributed through META-SHARE. For our conversation we can identify the following categories that impose different treatment as

[21]The list of RDF licenses can be checked at http://rdflicense.appspot.com/

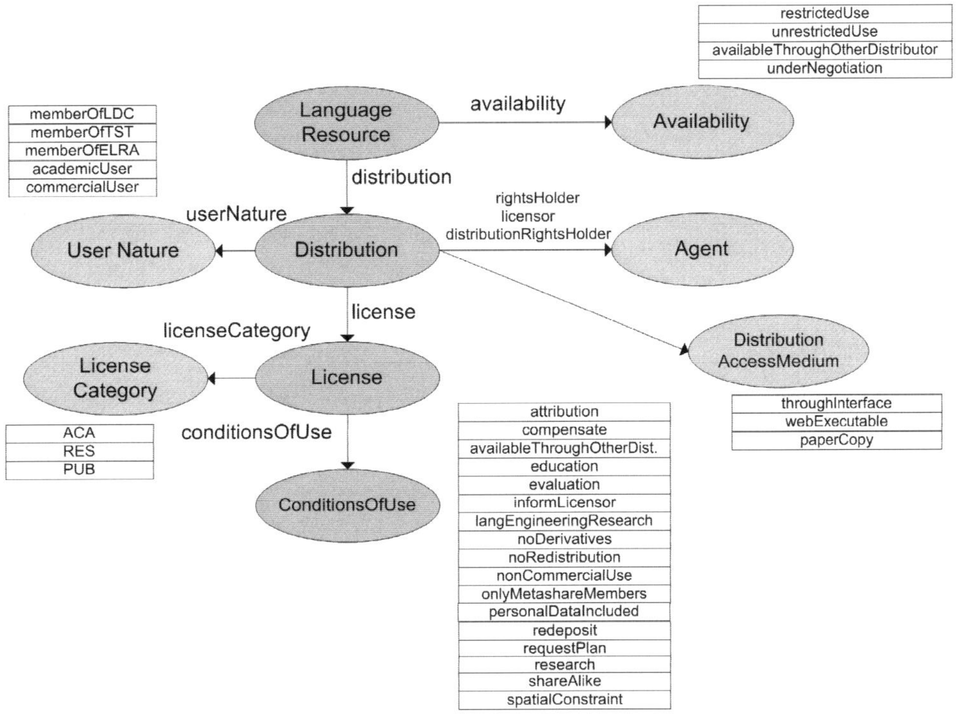

Figure 4: Rights Information for Language Resources

regards their RDF representation:

- Licenses, such as CC and FOSS that do not require any signatures; they are legal documents with a general text specifying the offering terms for end-users, they apply to all and do not ask for formal commitments from them. The text is published on a web site and can be accessed by anyone. They can have a direct representation in RDF.

- Standard licenses that include instantiation elements (e.g. ELRA, META-SHARE): legal documents that need to be signed by both contracting parties; they consist of a general text but include also specific terms that must be instantiated for each LR: the LR identification data as well as those of the signatories, but also specific fields such as the amount to be paid, the place where the LR will be used etc.; the licenses are available over the internet and can be accessed by anyone. In this case, the general text can be represented in RDF but we separated what is particular to the resource (e.g. the amount of money) and what is general and can be included in the RDF of the license (e.g. the obligation to pay). For example, in order to declare that a resource is distributed under a META-SHARE Commercial-NoRedistribution-ForAFee license, the RDF fragment in Figure 6 can be used in its metadata record. The first line declares that *:resource* is a *dcat:Distribution*. The Dublin Core *license*[22] property links the resource with the license, and the price -whose precise number is not specific in the generic license online- is given. The price is specified using the GoodRelations[23] vocabulary.

- License templates with potential extra terms (e.g. CLARIN [24]): legal documents that include a general text and extra potential terms (e.g. attribution, request for a research plan, usage of the resource only at a specific location etc.); i.e. the use or not of specific terms leads to a new combination and the creation of a new license. The texts are also avail-

[22]dct is the prefix of http://purl.org/dc/terms/

[23]www.heppnetz.de/projects/goodrelations/

[24]http://clarin.eu/content/licenses-agreements-legal-terms

```
:resource a dcat:Distribution ;
 dct:license <http://purl.org/NET/
 rdflicense/ms-c-nored-ff> ;
 gr:hasPriceSpecification [
  gr:hasCurrencyValue "400"^^xsd:float;
  gr:hasCurrency "USD"^^xsd:string
 ].
] .
```

Figure 6: Example showing the use of a license template

able over the internet, but the combinations of the terms are free. The basic text itself can be represented in RDF, and so can the terms but the full RDF representation of all combinations must be dynamically constructed, with a combination of the RDF representation of the general text and the RDF representations of each additional term, once this is selected.[25]

- Non-standard licenses, such as proprietary ones, legal notices, terms of use etc.: there's a large variety of them, not all of the texts are available over the internet. There cannot be a ready-made RDF representation available for all of them. In this case, the conditionsOfUse element can help the end users get a quick grasp of what they are allowed to do with the LR.

The next example, in Figure 8, shows unabridged the "META-SHARE Commercial No Redistribution" license. The main resource in the license is an *odrl:Policy* (line 02) which has attributed some metadata elements: version (03), label (04), alternative name (05) or location of the legal code[26] (10). The policy additionally has information regarding the language and a flat list with the conditions (*ms:NoRedistribution*, *cc:Attribution*, etc. in lines 07-09).

The main permission (lines 12-25), which explicitly authorizes for making derivative works, making commercial use has the duty of attribution (15-17) and the constraints of being used only for language engineering purposes (lines 18-21) and on the users' site (lines 21-24). Distribution is forbidden in lines 26-28.

[25]see, for instance, `https://www.clarin.eu/content/clarin-license-category-calculator` with possible combination of license categories and terms of use.

[26]cc is prefix of `http://creativecommons.org/ns#`

5 Conclusions and future work

This paper has presented the Rights Information for Language Resources Ontology, the outcome of a cooperation between the META-SHARE project and the LIDER project, in the framework of the W3C Linked Data for Language Technology Group, which is expected to enhance the accessibility of language resources, following the Linked Data model, and facilitate their automatic processing by web services.

In the future, we expect to improve on the model, especially as regards the user modelling, as well as implement a mechanism for the dynamic generation of RDF representations of non-standard licences. Finally, the use of SPARQL queries to fill in predefined data structures will be investigated, so that the original ODRL structure is preserved while keeping the concept of license template.

Acknowledgments

We are very grateful to the members of the W3C Linked Data for Language Technology (LD4LT) for all the useful feedback received and for allowing this initiative to be developed as an activity of the group as well as the Legal Group at ILSP/RC Athena who have contributed with discussions for the overall schema. This work is supported by the FP7 European project LIDER (610782), by the Spanish Ministry of Economy and Competitiveness (project TIN2013-46238-C4-2-R and a Juan de la Cierva grant), the Greek CLARIN Attiki project (MIS 441451) and the H2020 project CRACKER (645357).

References

Daan Broeder, Menzo Windhouwer, Dieter Van Uytvanck, Twan Goosen, and Thorsten Trippel. 2012. CMDI: a component metadata infrastructure. In *Describing LRs with metadata: towards flexibility and interoperability in the documentation of LR workshop programme*, page 1.

Nicoletta Calzolari, Riccardo Del Gratta, Gil Francopoulo, Joseph Mariani, Francesco Rubino, Irene Russo, and Claudia Soria. 2012. The LRE Map. Harmonising community descriptions of resources. In *Proceedings of the Eighth Conference on International Language Resources and Evaluation*, pages 1084–1089.

Maria Gavrilidou, Penny Labropoulou, Elina Desipri, Stelios Piperidis, Haris Papageorgiou, Mon-

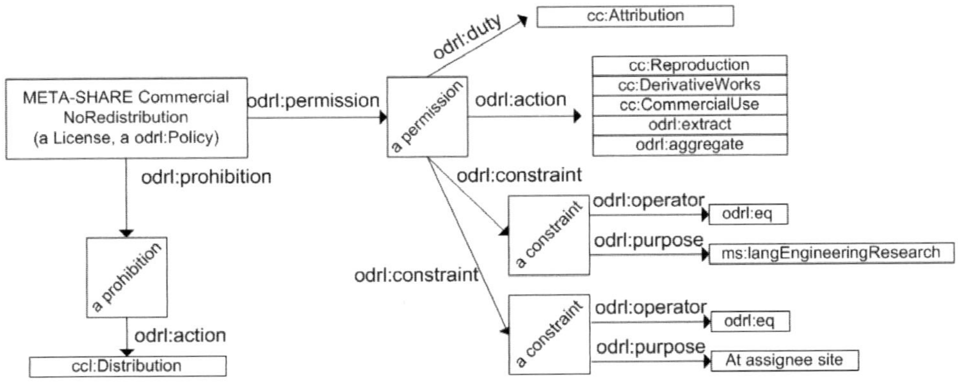

Figure 7: Graphical representation of the license in Figure 8

```
<http://purl.org/NET/rdflicense/ms-c-nored>
 a odrl:Policy ;
 dct:hasVersion "1.0" ;
 rdfs:label "META-SHARE Commercial NoRedistribution" ;
 dct:alternative "MS C-NoReD" ;
 dct:language <http://www.lexvo.org/page/iso639-3/eng> ;
 ms:conditionsOfUse ms:noRedistribution, cc:Attribution,
   cc:CommercialUse, ms:conditionsOfUse,
   ms:languageEngineeringResearch ;
 cc:legalcode <http://www.meta-net.eu/meta-s[...etc...].pdf> .
 ms:licenseCategory ms:PUB ;
 odrl:permission [
    odrl:action cc:Reproduction, cc:DerivativeWorks , odrl:extract,
        odrl:aggregate, cc:CommercialUse ;
    odrl:duty [
 odrl:action cc:Attribution ;
    ] ;
    odrl:constraint [
      odrl:operator odrl:eq ;
      odrl:purpose ms:languageEngineeringResearch
    ] , [
      odrl:operator odrl:eq ;
      odrl:spatial "only at assignee's site"
    ]
 ];
 odrl:prohibition [
    odrl:action cc:Distribution ;
 ] .
```

Figure 8: The META-SHARE Commercial No-redistribution license

ica Monachini, Francesca Frontini, Thierry Declerck, Gil Francopoulo, Victoria Arranz, and Valrie Mapelli. 2012. The META-SHARE metadata schema for the description of language resources. In *Proceedings of the Eighth International Conference on Language Resources and Evaluation*, pages 1090–1097.

John McCrae, Penny Labropoulou, Jorge Gracia, Marta Villegas, Victor Rodriguez-Doncel, and Philipp Cimiano. 2015. One ontology to bind them all: The META-SHARE OWL ontology for the interoperability of linguistic datasets on the Web. In *Proceedings of the 4th Workshop on the Multilingual Semantic Web (to appear).*

Mo McRoberts and Victor Rodriguez-Doncel (eds.). 2015. ODRL Version 2.1 Ontology. Final specification, ODRL W3C Community Group, March. http://www.w3.org/ns/odrl/2/.

Ville Oksanen and Crister Lindn. 2011. Open content licenses - how to choose the right one. In *NEALT Proceedings Series Vol. 13.*

Stelios Piperidis. 2012. The META-SHARE language resources sharing infrastructure: Principles, challenges, solutions. In *Proceedings of the Eighth Conference on International Language Resources and Evaluation*, pages 36–42.

Victor Rodriguez-Doncel, Serena Villata, and Asuncion Gomez-Perez. 2014. A dataset of RDF licenses. In Rinke Hoekstra, editor, *Proceedings of the 27th International Conference on Legal Knowledge and Information System*, pages 187–189.

Gary Simons and Steven Bird. 2003. Building an open language archives community on the oai foundation. *Library Hi Tech*, 21(2):210–218.

Claudia Soria, Nicoletta Calzolari, Monica Monachini, Valeria Quochi, Nria Bel, Khalid Choukri, Joseph Mariani, Jan Odijk, and Stelios Piperidis. 2014. The language resource strategic agenda: the flarenet synthesis of community recommendations. *Language Resources and Evaluation*, 48(4):753–775.

Marta Villegas, Maite Melero, and Nuria Bel. 2014. Metadata as Linked Open Data: mapping disparate XML metadata registries into one RDF/OWL registry. In *Proceedings of LREC 2014.*

Linking four heterogeneous language resources as linked data

Benjamin Siemoneit, John P. McCrae, Philipp Cimiano
Cognitive Interaction Technology, Center of Excellence, Bielefeld University
Bielefeld, Germany
bsiemone@techfak.uni-bielefeld.de
{jmccrae,cimiano}@cit-ec.uni-bielefeld.de

Abstract

The interest in publishing language resources as linked data is increasing, as clearly corroborated by the recent growth of the Linguistic Linked Data cloud. However, the actual value of data published as linked data is the fact that it is linked across datasets, supporting integration and discovery of data. As the manual creation of links between datasets is costly and therefore does not scale well, automatic linking approaches are of great importance to increase the quality and degree of linking of the Linguistic Linked Data cloud. In this paper we examine an automatic approach to link four different datasets to each other: two terminologies, the *European Migration Network (EMN)* glossary as well as the *Interactive Terminology for Europe* (IATE), BabelNet, and the Manually Annotated Subcorpus (MASC) of the American National Corpus. We describe our methodology, present some results on the quality of the links and summarize our experiences with this small linking exercise We will make sure that the resources are added to the linguistic linked data cloud.

1 Introduction

Linked data has recently become a popular approach to publishing language resources on the Web. It has been argued (Chiarcos et al., 2013) that the linked data approach applied to language resources has important advantages, most notably its ability to break the limitations of classical resource types and to foster integration of data by linking data across resources.

As the manual creation of links between datasets is costly and therefore does not scale well, automatic linking approaches are of great importance to increase the quality and degree of linking of the Linguistic Linked Data cloud. In this paper we describe the results of a small project attempting to link four datasets of different types (two terminologies, one lexico-conceptual resource and one corpus). As terminological resources, we have considered the Glossary of the European Migration Network (EMN)[1] as well as the Interactive Terminology for Europe (IATE) [2]. They are both represented using the *lemon* model (McCrae et al., 2012). As lexico-conceptual resource we rely on BabelNet (Navigli and Ponzetto, 2012), which has been previously migrated into Linked Data (Ehrmann et al., 2014). As corpus we use the Manually Annotated Subcorpus (MASC) of the American National Corpus (Ide et al., 2008), which contains disambiguated links to BabelNet.

We describe how the datasets have been migrated to RDF and describe our methodology for linking the datasets at the lexical entry level and present a sampled evaluation of the quality of the induced links. We first use a simple technique based on strict matching of the canonical form of lexical entries in different resources. By this we then link the EMN to both IATE and BabelNet. MASC has been previously linked to BabelNet and we included these links into our version of MASC.

The paper is structured as follows: in the next Section 2 we briefly describe the models that have been used to represented the data as Linked Data. Section 3 describes how the datasets have been converted into RDF. Section 4 describes our methodology for linking and presents a sampled evaluation of the quality of the automatically induced links.

[1] http://ec.europa.eu/dgs/home-affairs/what-we-do/networks/european_migration_network/glossary/index_a_en.htm
[2] http://iate.europa.eu/

Proceedings of the 4th Workshop on Linked Data in Linguistics (LDL-2015), pages 59–63,
Beijing, China, July 31, 2015.

2 Models

We used two models to represent the datasets presented in this paper. The terminologies and dictionaries have been represented in RDF using the *lemon* model (Lexicon Model for Ontologies) (McCrae et al., 2012), which has been designed to represent lexical information relative to ontologies and other semantic structures such as terminologies. For the MASC corpus we used the NLP Interchange Format (NIF) (Hellmann et al., 2013), a stand-off annotation format for the representation of annotations of text for NLP applications. We briefly describe these models in the following:

2.1 Lemon-OntoLex

The *lemon* (Lexicon Model for Ontologies) was proposed by McCrae et al. (McCrae et al., 2012) as a model for the representation of lexical information and has more recently been as a basis for the standardization work of the W3C Community Group on Ontology-Lexica.[3] The model revolves around the key concept of a *lexical entry*, which consists of a number of *forms* (e.g., 'plural form'), having different written or phonetic representations. The meaning of the lexical entry is specified by *reference* to some ontological concept. This relation is mediated by a *lexical sense*. In the case of the terminological resources EMN and IATE we model each terminological concept as a `skos:Concept` and model each term as a lexical entry that has the corresponding `skos:Concept` as *reference*.

2.2 NIF

Modelling corpus data such as MASC requires that we are capable of representing the annotations of this data in a compact and effective manner. The NLP Interchange Format (NIF) supports the annotation of text by using stand-off annotations represented as RDF. For this, it reifies strings in the document as RDF resources that refer to a specific character offset. For example, the URI `http://www.example.com/document.txt#char=3,7` would refer to the word occurring in the document which can be found at the path and server given in the URI, the fragment identifier follows RFC 5417 (Wilde, 2008) and identifies the word between the 3rd and 7th character. This annotation object can then be further annotated with properties from NIF such as the start and end index (to enable direct querying) or annotations from other schemas suitable for this corpus.

[3] `http://www.w3.org/community/ontolex`

Resource	Size	Triples
IATE	8,081,142 terms	74,023,248
EMN	8,855 terms	106,283
MASC	506,768 words	8,650,723

Table 1: Size of the resources described in this paper without linking annotations.

3 Transformation to Linked Data

In this section we describe the transformation of the different datasets to RDF. The sizes of the resulting resources are given in Table 1 and are available for download at:

IATE `http://tbx2rdf.lider-project.eu/data/iate/`

EMN `http://data.lider-project.eu/emn/`

MASC `http://data.lider-project.eu/MASC-NIF/`

BabelNet `http://babelnet.org/rdf/`

The original data resources were primarily available as XML documents and thus conversion was for the most part the straightforward task of matching elements in an XML scheme to a appropriate RDF constructs. This was done by means of developing converters that parsed the XML and generated appropriate RDF. We will describe the details of the mapping in the next sections.

3.1 Transformation of EMN

The EMN glossary consists of 388 entries related to asylum and migration. Each entry is comprised of an English term with translations into 22 EU languages, a concept definition, semantic relations to other entries, explanatory comments and the source of the definition. We extracted the glossary from the HTML and converted it into linked data he *lemon* model.

A *lemon* `Lexicon` was created for each language. Then, for each EMN entry and for each of the available translations, a `LexicalEntry` was added to the respective `Lexicon`.

In *lemon*, `LexicalSense` objects are used for mapping terms to ontological entities. Although EMN entries are not RDF resources, we attached

the URL of the respective entry as ontological reference to each sense.
The terms in EMN are not directly lemmas and so in order to incorporate them in a lexicon such as *lemon* we performed some preprocessing steps in order to obtain proper lexical entries: All additional information given in brackets or separated by special characters have been removed. The resulting strings were added as `LexicalForm` to their corresponding `LexicalEntry` objects.

3.2 Transformation of MASC

MASC contains 500K words of written and transcribed spoken language. Annotations for a variety of phenomena including BabelNet synset annotations are available in the Graph Annotation Format (GrAF) (Ide and Suderman, 2007). GrAF defines an XML serialization of graphs containing linguistic annotations. Graphs can, for example, be used to model the syntactic structure of the data, with nodes representing sentences, phrases etc. Leaf nodes refer to tokens in the primary data. Annotations can be attached to nodes and edges as feature structures.
In order to convert the corpus to NIF we first created a `nif:Context` for each primary data document. Nodes were then mapped to `nif:String` objects with normal RDF properties for a) a reference to the respective context object, b) the start and end indices of the chunk, c) the string representation of the chunk and d) all feature-value-pairs attached to the node.

3.3 Transformation of IATE

The IATE terminology is published using the TermBase Exchange (TBX, ISO 30042). We used the converter available under [4] to convert the IATE terminology into lemon-based RDF. As for EMN, terminological concepts were mapped to `skos:Concepts` and terms were mapped to lexical entries referring to the corresponding concept. In the IATE dataset, each concept has a *reliability code* and *subject field*, which were also represented as RDF. The language codes of terms were mapped to LexVo (de Melo, 2015) URIs.

4 Linking

4.1 Linking EMN to IATE

Concepts in the EMN datasets were linked to concepts in IATE by matching the written representation of the corresponding lexical entries in different languages. The number of languages for which the lexical entries for a given concept match was regarded as an indicator of the quality of the match, that is the more languages yield a match, the higher the quality of the induced link was expected to be.

In particular, EMN concepts were linked to IATE concepts by searching for string matches between corresponding EMN lexical entries and IATE lexical entries in multiple languages. In order to improve recall, we used Snowball stemming[5] for the eleven supported EU languages and transformed all strings to lowercase. The search was limited to IATE concepts associated with migration (subject field 2811).
Multiple IATE concepts can match a single EMN concept. In order to decide between candidate matches, we counted the number of languages for which each match holds and used this count as a measure for match plausibility (see Figure 1). We induced 3,028 links between EMN and IATE by considering all possible matches. Only considering the best match for each EMN concept resulted in 2,038 links (compare Table 2).

Resources	Number of links	Percentage of EMN	Precision
EMN-BabelNet	1,347	15%	69%
EMN-IATE (all matches)	3,082	35%	93%
EMN-IATE (best matches)	2,038	23%	94%

Table 2: Number of links between resources and precision of mapping.

4.2 Linking EMN to BabelNet

EMN concepts were linked to BabelNet by using the Babelfy (Moro et al., 2014) named entity linking service. Invoking the Babelfy disambiguation algorithm on the written representation of the lexical entries, we extracted all the synsets that Babelfy annotated the written representation with and considered only those annotations consisting of exactly one synset. A precision of 69% was determined by manually comparing concept definitions for a sample of 100 matches.

[4] `https://github/cimiano/tbx2rdf`

[5] `http://snowball.tartarus.org/`

Resources	Number of links
IATE-EMN-BabelNet	700
EMN-BabelNet-MASC	37,405
IATE-EMN-BabelNet-MASC	7,794

Table 3: Number of transitive links added to resources.

On the basis of the existing linking between MASC and BabelNet and the above mentioned induced links between EMN and IATE (3,028, see Table 2) as well as between EMN and BabelNet (1,347, see Table 2), by transitive closure we were able to induce 700 links between IATE and BabelNet (via EMN as pivot), 37,405 links between EMN and MASC (via BabelNet as pivot) and 7,794 between IATE and MASC (via BabelNet and EMN as pivots). The results are summarized in Table 3.
To give an example, the EMN term 'visa' was linked to the matching term associated with IATE concept 3556819 and to BabelNet synset bn:00080087n, which in turn had been used to annotate 15 different tokens in MASC.

4.3 Linking precision

We evaluated the linking precision by manually evaluating a sample of 100 generated links. Precision of the linking is defined as the number of correctly created links divided by the number of generated links. Precision was determined by manually comparing terms, definitions and sources for a sample of matches: a link was judged as correct if the concepts share the same source or if their definitions don't contradict and there is no better matching concept.

The precision of the linking is shown in Table 2. The precision of linking EMN to IATE is quite high, which is due to the fact that they are terminologies and typically only contain one sense or meaning for a certain term / lexical entry. In contrast, BabelNet contains many possible senses for each lexical entry, so that the right sense among all the candidate senses needs to be found and this leads to errors.

We evaluated the precision of the induced links in dependence of the number of languages for which the written representations match. This analysis is shown in Figure 1. We observe that there is a clear improvement when considering links induced when the written representations for more than 5 languages match.

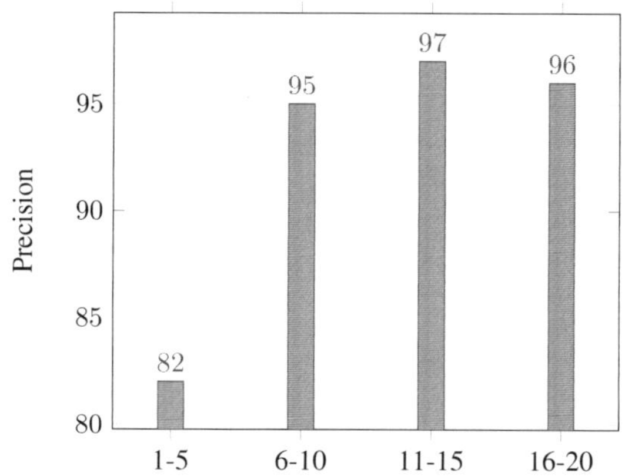

Figure 1: Precision of linking by number of languages matching for EMN-IATE mapping.

Finally, we evaluated the transitive linking and the results are presented in Table 3, we found that the two chains using one intermediate resource still maintained a large percentage of the links, as 52% of links from BabelNet to EMN could then be further extended to IATE. Furthermore, even using two intermediate resources still returned a useful number of links.

5 Conclusion

In this paper we have presented an experience report summarizing our experiences in developing an automatic approach to link four different language resources to each other. We have described a methodology that induces a link if the written representations of the lexical entries of the corresponding concepts match for a number of languages. We have shown that results are generally accurate, in particular when inducing links between terminologies. Further, the precision increases the more languages we require to have a match. Future work should be devoted to improving our methodology to increase both precision and recall of the generated links and thus reduce manual post-processing effort. Further, new methodologies for involving humans in the curation and validation of such links must be developed.

Acknowledgments

This work was funded under LIDER ("Linked Data as an enabler of cross-media and multilingual content analytics for enterprises across Europe"), an FP7 project refererence number 610782 in the topic ICT-2013.4.1: Content analytics and language technologies. This work was also funded as part of the Cluster of Excellence Cognitive Interaction Technology 'CITEC' (EXC 277), Bielefeld University.

References

Christian Chiarcos, John McCrae, Philipp Cimiano, and Christiane Fellbaum. 2013. Towards open data for linguistics: Lexical linked data. In *New Trends of Research in Ontologies and Lexical Resources*, pages 7–25. Springer.

Gerard de Melo. 2015. Lexvo. org: Language-related information for the linguistic linked data cloud. *Semantic Web*, 6(4).

Maud Ehrmann, Francesco Cecconi, Daniele Vannella, John P. McCrae, Philipp Cimiano, and Roberto Navigli. 2014. Representing multilingual data as linked data: the case of BabelNet 2.0. In *In Proceedings of the Ninth International Conference on Language Resources and Evaluation*, volume 14, pages 401–408.

Sebastian Hellmann, Jens Lehmann, Sören Auer, and Martin Brümmer. 2013. Integrating NLP using linked data. In *Proceedings of the 12th International Semantic Web Conference*, pages 98–113.

Nancy Ide and Keith Suderman. 2007. GrAF: A graph-based format for linguistic annotations. In *Proceedings of the Linguistic Annotation Workshop*, pages 1–8.

Nancy Ide, Collin Baker, Christiane Fellbaum, and Charles Fillmore. 2008. MASC: The manually annotated sub-corpus of American English. In *In Proceedings of the Sixth International Conference on Language Resources and Evaluation.*

John McCrae, Guadalupe Aguado-de Cea, Paul Buitelaar, Philipp Cimiano, Thierry Declerck, Asunción Gómez-Pérez, Jorge Gracia, Laura Hollink, Elena Montiel-Ponsoda, Dennis Spohr, et al. 2012. Interchanging lexical resources on the Semantic Web. *Language Resources and Evaluation*, 46(4):701–719.

Andrea Moro, Alessandro Raganato, and Roberto Navigli. 2014. Entity linking meets word sense disambiguation: A unified approach. *Transactions of the Association for Computational Linguistics*, 2:231–244.

Roberto Navigli and Simone Paolo Ponzetto. 2012. Babelnet: The automatic construction, evaluation and application of a wide-coverage multilingual semantic network. *Artificial Intelligence*, 193:217–250.

E. Wilde. 2008. URI fragment identifiers for text/plain media types. Technical report, Internet Engineering Task Force. RFC 5147.

EVALution 1.0: an Evolving Semantic Dataset for Training and Evaluation of Distributional Semantic Models

Enrico Santus
The Hong Kong Polytechnic University
Hong Kong
esantus@gmail.com

Frances Yung
Nara Institute of Science and Technology
Nara, Japan
pikyufrances-y@is.naist.jp

Alessandro Lenci
Universita di Pisa
Pisa, Italy
alessandro.lenci@ling.unipi.it

Chu-Ren Huang
The Hong Kong Polytechnic University
Hong Kong
churen.huang@polyu.edu.hk

Abstract

In this paper, we introduce EVALution 1.0, a dataset designed for the training and the evaluation of Distributional Semantic Models (DSMs). This version consists of almost 7.5K tuples, instantiating several semantic relations between word pairs (including *hypernymy*, *synonymy*, *antonymy*, *meronymy*). The dataset is enriched with a large amount of additional information (i.e. relation domain, word frequency, word POS, word semantic field, etc.) that can be used for either filtering the pairs or performing an in-depth analysis of the results. The tuples were extracted from a combination of ConceptNet 5.0 and WordNet 4.0, and subsequently filtered through automatic methods and crowdsourcing in order to ensure their quality. The dataset is freely downloadable[1]. An extension in RDF format, including also scripts for data processing, is under development.

1 Introduction

Distributional Semantic Models (DSMs) represent lexical meaning in vector spaces by encoding corpora derived word co-occurrences in vectors (Sahlgren, 2006; Turney and Pantel, 2010; Lapesa and Evert, 2014). These models are based on the assumption that meaning can be inferred from the contexts in which terms occur. Such assumption is typically referred to as the *distributional hypothesis* (Harris, 1954).

DSMs are broadly used in Natural Language Processing (NLP) because they allow systems to automatically acquire lexical semantic knowledge in a fully unsupervised way and they have been proved to outperform other semantic models in a large number of tasks, such as the measurement of lexical semantic similarity and relatedness. Their geometric representation of semantic distance (Zesch and Gurevych, 2006) allows its calculation through mathematical measures, such as the *vector cosine*.

A related but more complex task is the identification of semantic relations. Words, in fact, can be similar in many ways. *Dog* and *animal* are similar because the former is a specific kind of the latter (*hyponym*), while *dog* and *cat* are similar because they are both specific kinds of *animal* (*coordinates*). DSMs do not provide by themselves a principled way to single out the items linked by a specific relation.

Several distributional approaches have tried to overcome such limitation in the last decades. Some of them use word pairs holding a specific relation as seeds, in order to discover patterns in which other pairs holding the same relation are likely to occur (Hearst, 1992; Pantel and Pennacchiotti, 2006; Cimiano and Völker, 2005; Berland and Charniak, 1999). Other approaches rely on linguistically grounded unsupervised measures, which adopt different types of distance measures by selectively weighting the vectors features (Santus et al., 2014a; Santus et al., 2014b; Lenci and Benotto, 2012; Kotlerman et al., 2010; Clarke,

[1] The resource is available at http://colinglab.humnet.unipi.it/resources/ and at https://github.com/esantus

Proceedings of the 4th Workshop on Linked Data in Linguistics (LDL-2015), pages 64–69,
Beijing, China, July 31, 2015.

2009; Weeds et al., 2004; Weeds and Weir, 2003). Both the abovementioned approaches need to rely on datasets containing semantic relations for training and/or evaluation.

EVALution is a dataset designed to support DSMs on both processes. This version consists of almost 7.5K tuples, instantiating several semantic relations between word pairs (including *hypernymy*, *synonymy*, *antonymy*, *meronymy*). The dataset is enriched with a large amount of additional information (i.e. relation domain, word frequency, word POS, word semantic field, etc.) that can be used for either filtering the pairs or performing an in-depth analysis of the results. The quality of the pairs is guaranteed by i.) their presence in previous resources, such as ConceptNet 5.0 (Liu and Singh, 2004) and WordNet 4.0 (Fellbaum, 1998), and ii.) a large agreement between native speakers (obtained in crowdsourcing tasks, performed with *Crowdflower*). In order to increase the homogeneity of the data and reduce its variability[2], the dataset only contains word pairs whose terms (henceforth *relata*) occur in more than one semantic relation. The additional information is provided for both *relata* and relations. Such information is based on both human judgments (e.g. relation domain, term generality, term abstractness, etc.) and on corpus data (e.g. frequency, POS, etc.).

2 Related Work

Up to now, DSMs performance has typically been evaluated against benchmarks developed for purposes other than DSMs evaluation. Except for BLESS (Baroni and Lenci, 2011), most of the adopted benchmarks include task-specific resources, such as the 80 multiple-choice synonym questions of the *Test of English as a Foreign Language* (*TOEFL*) (Landauer and Dumais, 1997), and general-purpose resources, such as WordNet (Fellbaum, 1998). None of them can be considered fully reliable for DSMs evaluation for several reasons: i.) general-purpose resources need to be inclusive and comprehensive, and therefore they either adopt broad definitions of semantic relations or leave them undefined, leading to inhomogeneous pairs; ii.) task-specific resources, on the other hand, adopt specific criteria for defining semantic relations, according to the scope of the resource (e.g. the word pairs may be more or less prototypical, according to the difficulty of the test); iii.) *relata* and relations are given without additional information, which is instead necessary for testing and analyze DSMs performance in a more detailed way (e.g. relation domain, word semantic field, word frequency, word POS, etc.).

Given its large size, in terms both of lexical items and coded relations, WordNet is potentially extremely relevant to evaluate DSMs. However, since it has been built by lexicographers without checking against human judgments, WordNet is not fully reliable as a gold standard. Moreover, the resource is also full with inconsistencies in the way semantic relations have been encoded. Simply looking at the hypernymy relation (Cruse, 1986), for example, we can see that it is used in both a taxonomical (i.e. *dog* is a hyponym of *animal*) and a vague and debatable way (i.e. *silly* is a hyponym of *child*). ConceptNet (Liu and Singh, 2004) may be considered even less homogeneous, given its size and the automatic way in which it was developed.

Landauer and Dumais (1997) introduces the 80 multiple-choice synonym questions of the *TOEFL* as a benchmark in the synonyms identification task. Although good results in such set (Rapp, 2003) may have a strong impact on the audience, its small size and the fact that it contains only synonyms cannot make it an accurate benchmark to evaluate DSMs.

For what concerns antonymy, based on similar principles to the *TOEFL*, Mohammed et al. (2008) proposes a dataset containing 950 closest-opposite questions, where five alternatives are provided for every target word. Their data are collected starting from 162 questions in the Graduate Record Examination (*GRE*).

BLESS (Baroni and Lenci, 2011) contains several relations, such as hypernymy, co-hyponymy, meronymy, event, attribute, etc. This dataset covers 200 concrete and unambiguous concepts divided in 17 categories (e.g. vehicle, ground mammal, etc.). Every concept is linked through the various semantic relations to several *relata* (which can be either nouns, adjectives or verbs). Unfortunately this dataset does not contain synonymy and antonymy related pairs.

With respect to entailment, Baroni et al.(2012)

[2]Reducing the variability should impact both on training and evaluation. In the former case, because it should help in identifying consistent patterns and discriminate them from the inconsistent ones. In the latter case, because it should allow meaningful comparisons of the results.

have built a dataset containing 1,385 positive (e.g. house-building) and negative (e.g. leader-rider) examples: the former are obtain by selecting particular hypernyms from WordNet, while the latter are obtained by randomly shuffling the hypernyms of the positive examples. The pairs are then manually double-checked.

Another resource for similarity is WordSim 353 (Finkelstein et al., 2002; Baroni and Lenci, 2011), which is built by asking subjects to rate the similarity in a set of 353 word pairs. While refining such dataset, Agirre (2009) found that several types of similarity are involved (i.e. he can recognize, among the others, hypernyms, coordinates, meronyms and topically related pairs).

Recently, Santus et al. (2014c; 2014b) use a subset of 2,232 English word pairs collected by Lenci/Benotto in 2012/13 through Amazon Mechanical Turk, following the method described by Scheible and Schulte im Walde (2014). Targets are balanced across word categories. Frequency and degree of ambiguity are also taken into consideration. The dataset includes hypernymy, antonymy and synonymy for nouns, adjectives and verbs.

The constant need for new resources has recently led Gheorghita and Pierrel (2012) to suggest an automatic method to build a hypernym dataset by extracting hypernyms from definitions in dictionaries. A precision of 72.35% is reported for their algorithm.

3 Design, Method and Statistics

As noted by Hendrickx et al. (2009), an ideal dataset for semantic relations should be exhaustive and mutually exclusive. That is, every word pair should be related by one, and only one, semantic relation. Unfortunately, such ideal case is very far from reality. Relations are ambiguous, hard to define and generally context-dependent (e.g. *hot* and *warm* may either be synonyms or antonyms, depending on the context).

EVALution is designed to reduce such issues by providing i.) consistent data, ii.) prototypical pairs and iii.) additional information. The first requirement is achieved by selecting only word pairs whose *relata* occur (independently) in more than one semantic relation, so that the variability in the data is drastically reduced. This should both improve the training process (being *relata* in more relations, the pairs can be used not only to find new patterns, but also to discriminate the ambiguous patterns from the safe ones) and the evaluation (allowing significant comparisons among the results). The second requirement is achieved by selecting only the pairs that obtain a large agreement between native speakers (judgments are collected in crowdsourcing tasks, performed with *Crowdflower*). Finally, the third requirement is achieved by providing additional information obtained through both human judgments (e.g. relation domain, term generality, term abstractness, etc.) and corpus-based analysis (e.g. frequency, POS, etc.).

3.1 Methodology

EVALution 1.0 is the result of a combination and filtering of ConceptNet 5.0 (Liu and Singh, 2004) and WordNet 4.0 (Fellbaum, 1998). Two kinds of filtering are applied: automatic filters and native speakers judgments. Automatic filtering is mainly intended to remove tuples including: i.) non-alphabetical terms; ii.) relations that are not relevant (see Table 1[3]); iii.) pairs that already appear in inverted order; iv.) pairs whose *relata* did not appear in at least 3 relations; v.) pairs that are already present in the BLESS and in the Lenci/Benotto datasets.

Relation	Pairs	*Relata*	Sentence template
IsA (hypernym)	1880	1296	X is a kind of Y
Antonym	1600	1144	X can be used as the opposite of Y
Synonym	1086	1019	X can be used with the same meaning of Y
Meronym	1003	978	X is ...
- PartOf	654	599	... part of Y
- MemberOf	32	52	... member of Y
- MadeOf	317	327	...made of Y
Entailment	82	132	If X is true, than also Y is true
HasA (possession)	544	460	X can have or can contain Y
HasProperty (attribute)	1297	770	Y is to specify X

Table 1: Relations, number of pairs, number of *relata* and sentence templates

Native speakers judgments are then collected

[3]For the definition of the semantic relations, visit: https://github.com/commonsense/conceptnet5/wiki/Relations

for the about 13K automatically filtered pairs. We create a task in *Crowdflower*, asking subjects to rate from 1 (Strongly disagree) to 5 (Strongly agree) the truth of sentences containing the target word pairs (e.g. dog *is a kind of* animal). We collect 5 judgments per sentence. Only pairs that obtain at least 3 positive judgments are included in the dataset. Table 1 summarizes the number of pairs per relation that passed this threshold and provides the sentence templates used to collect the judgments.

For the selected pairs and their *relata*, we perform two more crowdsourcing tasks, asking subjects to tag respectively the contexts/domains in which the sentences are true and the categories of the *relata*. Subjects are allowed to select one or more tags for each instance. For every *relatum*, we collect tags from 2 subjects, while for every pair we collect tags from 5 subjects. Table 2 contains the set of available tags for both relations and *relata*, and their distribution (only tags that were selected at least twice are reported).

3.2 Statistics

The dataset contains 7,429 word pairs, involving 1,829 *relata* (63 of which are multiword expressions). On average, every *relatum* occurs in 3.2 relations and every relation counts 644 *relata* (see Table 1).

For every *relatum*, the dataset contains four types of corpus-based metadata, including lemma frequency, POS distribution, inflection distribution and capitalization distribution. Such data is extracted from a combination of ukWaC and WaCkypedia (Santus et al., 2014a). Finally, for every relation and *relata*, descriptive tags collected through the crowdsourcing task described above are provided together with the number of subjects that have choosen them out of the total number of annotators. Table 2 describes the distribution of the tags.

4 Evaluation

In order to further evaluate the dataset, we built a 30K dimensions standard window-based matrix, recording co-occurrences with the nearest 2 content words to the left and the right of the target. Co-occurrences are extracted from a combination of the freely available ukWaC and WaCkypedia corpora (Santus et al., 2014a) and weighted with Local Mutual Information (LMI). We then calculate the *vector cosine* values for all the pairs in EVALution and for all those in BLESS (for comparison). Figure 1 shows the box-plots summarizing their distribution per relation.

Relation tag	**Distr.**	***Relata* tags**	**Distr.**
Event	2711	Basic/	382
		Subordinate/	163
		Superordinate	186
Time	266	General	565
		Specific	221
Space	962	Abstract/	430
		Concrete	531
Object	3011	Event	225
Nature	2372	Time	20
Culture	861	Space	115
Emotion	1005	Object	223
Relationship	1552	Animal	52
Communication	567	Plant	23
Food	404	Food	52
Color	269	Color	20
Business	245	People	100

Table 2: The distribution of tags for relations and *relata* (only tags that were selected at least twice are reported). Every relation and *relatum* can have more than one tag.

4.1 Discussion

As shown in Figure 1, the *vector cosine* values are higher for antonymy, possession (*HasA*), hypernymy (*IsA*), member-of, part-of and synonymy. This result is quite expected for synonyms, antonyms and hypernyms (Santus et al., 2014a; Santus et al., 2014b) and it is not surprising for member-of (e.g. star *MemberOf* constellation), part-of (e.g. word *PartOf* phrase) and possession (e.g. arm *HasA* hand). The *vector cosine* values are instead lower for entailment, attribute (*HasProperty*) and made-of, which generally involve *relata* that are semantically more distant.

In general, we can say that the variance between the distributions of *vector cosine* values per relation is low. This is however very similar to what happens with BLESS, where only coordinate and random pairs are significantly different, demonstrating once more that the *vector cosine* is not sufficient to discriminate semantic relations.

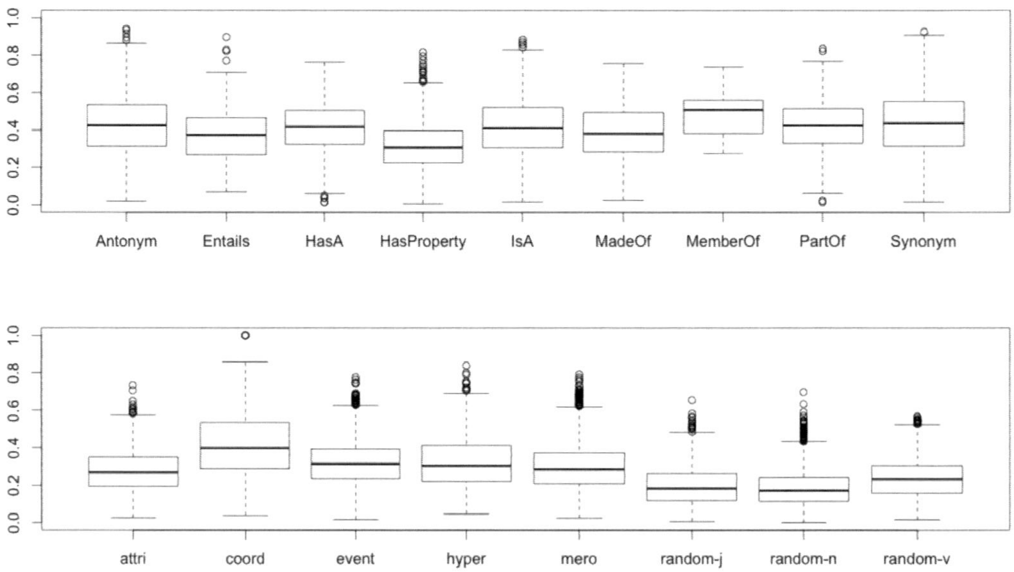

Figure 1: Distribution of vector cosine values in EVALution (above) and BLESS (below)

5 Conclusion and Future Work

EVALution is designed as an evolving dataset including tuples representing semantic relations between word pairs. Compared to previous resources, it is characterized by i.) internal consistency (i.e. few terms occurring in more relationships); ii.) prototypical pairs (i.e. high native speakers agreement, collected through crowdsourcing judgments); iii.) a large amount of additional information that can be used for further data filtering and analysis. Finally, it is freely available online at http://colinglab.humnet.unipi.it/resources/ and at https://github.com/esantus.

Further work is aiming to improve and extend the resource. This would require further quality-checks on data and metadata, the addition of new pairs and extra information, and the adoption of a format (such as RDF) that would turn our dataset into an interoperable linked open data. We are currently considering the *LEMON* model, which was previously used to encode BabelNet 2.0 (Ehrmann et al., 2014) and WordNet (McCrae et al., 2014). Some scripts will also be added for helping analyzing DSMs performance.

Acknowledgement

This work is partially supported by HK PhD Fellowship Scheme under PF12-13656.

References

Eneko Agirre, Enrique Alfonseca, Keith Hall, Jana Kravalova, Marius Paşca, and Aitor Soroa. 2009. A study on similarity and relatedness using distributional and wordnet-based approaches. *Proceedings of the Annual Conference of the North American Chapter of the Association for Computational Linguistics.*

Marco Baroni and Alessandro Lenci. 2011. How we blessed distributional semantic evaluation. *Proceedings of the Workshop on Geometrical Models of Natural Language Semantics.*

Marco Baroni, Raffaella Bernardi, Ngoc-Quynh Do, and Chung chieh Shan. 2012. Entailment above the word level in distributional semantics. *Proceedings of the Conference of the European Chapter of the Association for Computational Linguistics.*

Mathew Berland and Eugene Charniak. 1999. Finding parts in very large corpora. *Proceedings of the Annual Meeting of the Association for Computational Linguistics.*

Philipp Cimiano and Johanna Völker. 2005. text2onto. *Natural language processing and information systems.*

Daoud Clarke. 2009. Context-theoretic semantics for natural language: An overview. *Proceedings of the Workshop on Geometrical Models of Natural Language Semantics.*

D. Alan Cruse. 1986. *Lexical semantics.* Cambridge University Press.

Maud Ehrmann, Francesca Cecconi, Daniele Vannella, John P. McCrae, Philipp Cimiano, and Roberto Navigli. 2014. A multilingual semantic network as linked data: lemon-babelnet. *Proceedings of the Workshop on Linked Data in Linguistics*.

Christiane Fellbaum. 1998. *Wordnet*. Wiley Online Library.

Lev Finkelstein, Evgeniy Gabrilovich, Yossi Matias, Ehud Rivlin, Zach Solan, Gadi Wolfman, and Eytan Ruppin. 2002. Placing search in context: The concept revisited. *ACM Transactions on Information Systems,*.

Inga Gheorghita and Jean-Marie Pierrel. 2012. Towards a methodology for automatic identification of hypernyms in the definitions of large-scale dictionary. *Proceedings of the International Conference on Language Resources and Evaluation*.

Zellig S. Harris. 1954. Distributional structure. *Word*.

Marti A. Hearst. 1992. Automatic acquisition of hyponyms from large text corpora. *Proceedings of the International Conference on Computational Linguistics*.

Iris Hendrickx, Su Nam Kim, Zornitsa Kozareva, Preslav Nakov, Diarmuid Ó Séaghdha, Sebastian Padó, Marco Pennacchiotti, Lorenza Romano, and Stan Szpakowicz. 2009. Multi-way classification of semantic relations between pairs of nominals. *Proceedings of the Workshop on Semantic Evaluations*.

Lili Kotlerman, Ido Dagan, Idan Szpektor, and Maayan Zhitomirsky-Geffet. 2010. Directional distributional similarity for lexical inference. *Natural Language Engineering*.

Thomas K. Landauer and Susan T. Dumais. 1997. A solution to plato's problem: The latent semantic analysis theory of acquisition, induction, and representation of knowledge. *Psychological Review*.

Gabriella Lapesa and Stefan Evert. 2014. A large scale evaluation of distributional semantic models: Parameters, interactions and model selection. *Transactions of the Association for Computational Linguistics*.

Alessandro Lenci and Giulia Benotto. 2012. Identifying hypernyms in distributional semantic spaces. *Proceedings of the First Joint Conference on Lexical and Computational Semantics*.

Hugo Liu and Push Singh. 2004. Conceptnet—a practical commonsense reasoning tool-kit. *BT Technology Journal*.

John P. McCrae, Christiane D. Fellbaum, and Philipp Cimiano. 2014. Publishing and linking wordnet using lemon and rdf. *Proceedings of the Workshop on Linked Data in Linguistics*.

Saif Mohammad, Bonnie Dorr, and Graeme Hirst. 2008. Computing word-pair antonymy. *Proceedings of the Conference on Empirical Methods in Natural Language Processing*.

Patrick Pantel and Marco Pennacchiotti. 2006. Espresso: Leveraging generic patterns for automatically harvesting semantic relations. *Proceedings of the International Conference on Computational Linguistics and the Annual Meeting of the Association for Computational Linguistics*.

Reinhard Rapp. 2003. Word sense discovery based on sense descriptor dissimilarity. *Proceedings of Machine Translation Summit*.

Magnus Sahlgren. 2006. The word-space model: Using distributional analysis to represent syntagmatic and paradigmatic relations between words in high-dimensional vector spaces.

Enrico Santus, Alessandro Lenci, Qin Lu, and Sabine Schulte Im Walde. 2014a. Chasing hypernyms in vector spaces with entropy. *Proceedings of the Conference of the European Chapter of the Association for Computational Linguistics*.

Enrico Santus, Qin Lu, Alessandro Lenci, and Chu-Ren Huang. 2014b. Taking antonymy mask off in vector space. *Proceedings of the Pacific Asia Conference on Language, Information and Computing*.

Enrico Santus, Qin Lu, Alessandro Lenci, and Chu-Ren Huang. 2014c. Unsupervised antonym-synonym discrimination in vector space. *Proceedings of the Italian Conference on Computational Linguistics*.

Silke Scheible and Sabine Schulte Im Walde. 2014. A database of paradigmatic semantic relation pairs for german nouns, verbs, and adjectives. *Proceedings of the Workshop on Lexical and Grammatical Resources for Language Processing*.

Peter D. Turney and Patrick Pantel. 2010. From frequency to meaning: Vector space models of semantics. *Journal of Artificial Intelligence Research*.

Julie Weeds and David Weir. 2003. A general framework for distributional similarity. *Proceedings of the Conference on Empirical Methods in Natural Language Processing*.

Julie Weeds, David Weir, and Dianna McCarthy. 2004. Characterising measures of lexical distributional similarity. *Proceedings of the International Conference on Computational Linguistics*.

Torsten Zesch and Iryna Gurevych. 2006. Automatically creating datasets for measures of semantic relatedness. *Proceedings of the Workshop on Linguistic Distances*.

Linguistic Linked Data in Chinese: The Case of Chinese Wordnet

Chih-Yao Lee
Graduate Institute of Linguistics,
National Taiwan University, Taiwan
chihyaolee@gmail.com

Shu-Kai Hsieh
Graduate Institute of Linguistics,
National Taiwan University, Taiwan
shukai@gmail.com

Abstract

The present study describes recent developments of Chinese Wordnet, which has been reformatted using the *lemon* model and published as part of the Linguistic Linked Open Data Cloud. While *lemon* suffices for modeling most of the structures in Chinese Wordnet at the lexical level, the model does not allow for finer-grained distinction of a word sense, or meaning facets, a linguistic feature also attended to in Chinese Wordnet. As for the representation of synsets, we use the WordNet RDF ontology for integration's sake. Also, we use another ontology proposed by the Global WordNet Association to show how Chinese Wordnet as Linked Data can be integrated into the Global WordNet Grid.

1 Introduction

Although the rationale underlying synsets remains disputable (Maziarz et al., 2013), the practical value of wordnet as lexical resource is undeniable, particularly that of the first and foremost of its kind, Princeton WordNet (PWN) (Fellbaum, 1998). According to a search run by Morato et al. (Morato et al., 2004) on some major bibliographic databases like LISA, INSPEC and IEEE, the decade between 1994 and 2003 saw a wide range of wordnet applications, including conceptual disambiguation, information retrieval, query expansion and machine translation, among others. At present, more than another decade after the survey, wordnets not only continue to assist in a variety of NLP tasks, but plays an important role in shaping the Semantic Web (Berners-Lee et al., 2001) along with other major language resources (De Melo, 2008).

Central to the practice of the Semantic Web is the use of Linked Data to harmonize and interlink resources and datasets on the Web. This idea has found its way into the world of linguistics and led to the emergence of the Linguistic Linked Open Data (LLOD) cloud (Chiarcos et al., 2011). Among the models available for lexicon representation, the *lemon* model (McCrae et al., 2012) is chosen. In adopting *lemon*, we intend not only to render Chinese Wordnet more accessible as Linked Data, but also to examine to what extent the model can express linguistic features peculiar to Chinese languages. On the other hand, we represent synsets using the WordNet RDF ontology designed by Princeton for use in the context of *lemon*. Finally, another ontology consisting of 71 Base Types proposed by the Global WordNet Association is used to illustrate how in the long run Chinese Wordnet can be integrated into the Global WordNet Grid (Pease et al., 2008).

2 Chinese Wordnet

Chinese Wordnet (CWN) is a lexical-conceptual network for Mandarin Chinese, its contents structured along the same lines of PWN. First constructed based on translational equivalents of PWN mapped to Suggested Upper Merged Ontology (Huang et al., 2004), CWN has been reconstructed from scratch in 2014 and released with an open-source license. As with most wordnets CWN provides knowledge about lexicalized concepts, including their representing lexical item's part-of-speech, definition, and a set of other lexicalized concepts with which they form a synset. To date, CWN contains more than 28,000 word-sense pairs that are organized in some 20,000 synsets. In addition to the synonymy implicitly present in synsets, CWN includes other lexical-semantic relations to connect the lexicalized concepts, meronomy and hypernymy-hyponymy in particular.

What distinguishes CWN from its counterparts for other languages are primarily the distinction of meaning facets (Ahrens et al., 1998; Hsieh, 2011)

Proceedings of the 4th Workshop on Linked Data in Linguistics (LDL-2015), pages 70–74,
Beijing, China, July 31, 2015.

and a newly conceived type of relation termed *paranymy* (Huang et al., 2007). However, it is to be revealed that the current design of *lemon* does not allow for the representation of meaning facets and that the vocabulary of WordNet RDF ontology does not include *paranymy*.

3 Converting CWN into Linked Data with *lemon*

To improve its interoperability with other lexical resources, CWN is converted in RDF format using the *lemon* model. The following subsections provide a general introduction to *lemon* and Linked Data, followed by a discussion of the idiosyncrasies of Mandarin (as reflected in CWN) to be considered for a thorough conversion to a linked, *lemon*ized version of CWN.

3.1 The *lemon* Model and CWN

lemon (McCrae et al., 2011) is an ontology-lexicon model for representing lexical resources whose semantics is given by an external ontology. Following the principle of semantics by reference (Buitelaar, 2010), the model is meant to allow for linguistic grounding of a given ontology via supplementing the ontology with information about how the elements in the ontology's vocabulary are lexicalized in a given natural language. With the lexical and semantic layers separated as such, the same *lemon*-based lexicon can describe elements belonging to different ontologies; conversely, the same ontology can describe the semantics of all lexical resources in *lemon* format. As shown in Figure 1, the core of *lemon* includes:

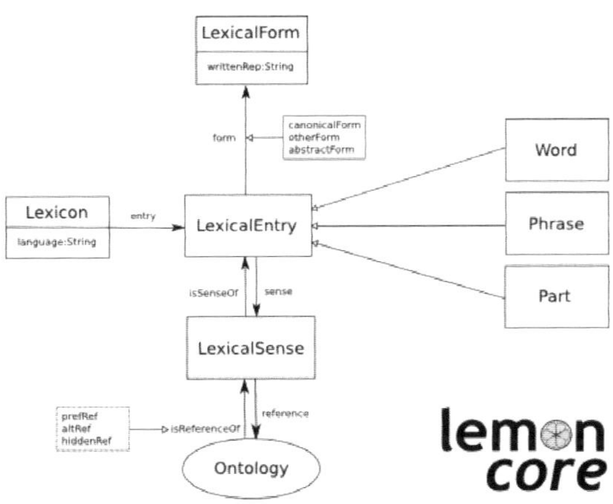

Figure 1: Core modules of the *lemon* model. (Taken from `http://lemon-model.net/`.)

- a *lexical entry*, which represents a single word or multi-word unit,
- a *lexical sense*, which represents the usage of a word as a *reference* to a concept in the ontology, and
- *forms*, which are inflected versions of the lexical entry, and associated with a string *representation*.

While *lemon* has proven adequate for modeling well-documented languages as those found in major lexical resources like PWN (McCrae et al., 2014) and Open Multilingual Wordnet (Bond and Foster, 2013), it remains to be seen whether the model is comprehensive enough for describing less privileged languages too. For instance, it is claimed that "the morphology module of *lemon* may serve less for Bantu languages lexica" (Chavula and Keet, 2014). In our case, while *lemon* suffices for modeling most of the structures in Chinese Wordnet at the lexical level, it does not allow for the representation of meaning facets. Consider the different uses of the lemma *shu1* "book" in the following sentences adapted from Bond et al. (2014):

(1) bang1 wo3 na2 na4 ben3 shu1
help me take that CL book
'Pass me that book.'

(2) ta1 zai4 du2 na4 ben3 shu1
he PROG read that CL book
'He is reading that book.'

(3) na2 yi4 ben3 shu1 gei3 wo3 kan3
take one CL book give me read
'Pass me a book to read.'

The same lemma *shu1* "book" refers to a physical object in (1) but to the information contained in (2). While the two readings may be referred to as different word senses, there exist contexts that allow the co-existence of both readings, as in (3), where the lemma can be interpreted as a physical object as well as the information contained in that object. Meaning distinction as such is therefore considered a facet rather than a sense.

Within the *lemon* model, however, there is no module for modeling meaning facets as there are for representing word forms and word senses. As a result, as many as 6,000 meaning facets identified in Chinese Wordnet cannot be published as part of the Linked Data for the time being.

3.2 Linked Data and Chinese Languages

Linked Data refers to data accessible on the Web and compiled such that it is machine-readable, its meaning is defined explicitly, and it is interlinked with other external data sets. Berners-Lee (2006) provides a set of guidelines for publishing Linked Data:

1. Use URIs as names for things.
2. Use HTTP URIs so that people can look up those names.
3. When someone looks up a URI, provide useful information, using the standards (RDF, SPARQL).
4. Include links to other URIs, so that they can discover more things.

Straightforward as the instructions may seem, the first rule regarding URI-naming already poses problems for languages whose writing system is not the Latin alphabet. Consider the URI scheme for identifying lemmas of a specific part-of-speech in the online RDF version of WordNet by Princeton[1]:

`http://.../wn31/` **{lemma}-{pos}**

If CWN adopts the same scheme and fills in the lemma slot with Chinese characters and specifies a lexical category, URIs as such will be generated:

`http://.../cwn/lod/` **詞目-n**

While multilingual addresses are well supported in modern web browsers, such URIs mean little to non-Chinese reading users and can hinder other resource providers from mapping CWN entries with their own. Another solution is to romanize the characters and number their tones:

`http://.../cwn/lod/` **ci2mu4-n**

Due to the prevalence of homophones in Chinese, however, the alternative leads to another issue: there exist many heterographs distinguishable only by their logographic representations when no context is given. A romanized form like *ci2mu4* can be interpreted nominally as "shrine-tomb" (祠墓) or "Ibaraki city" (茨木) as well as "lemma" (詞目). As a result, the design of such URI scheme is not effective in identifying a specific lexical entry, at least not for Chinese.[2] On the other hand, the RDF version of WordNet found in lemonUby[3] points to lemmas using the following URI scheme:

`http://.../WN_LexicalEntry_` **{id}**

By contrast, lemonUby makes use of unique IDs in combination with the prefix *WN_LexicalEntry_* to ensure one-to-one correspondence between URIs and lexical entries. Truly unique lemma identifiers are derived as such, even though the scheme observes the first rule for serving Linked Data only loosely, in the sense that with the prefix as the sole meaningful component part and without a lexical form embedded in the URI, the naming does not shed much light on the entry being linked to.

To uniquely identify lemmas without trading off URI readability on the part of the end user, CWN points to lemma entries using both a romanized lexical form and a unique ID. Take for example the following URI:

`http://.../cwn/lod/` **ai4** / **067081**

While the ID 067081 alone suffices to pinpoint its associated lexical entry, *ai4* "love" helps indicate the phonetic form of the lemma being referred to. When the trailing ID is not specified, however, all the entries with the romanization *ai4* will be listed along with their respective IDs. The optionality of the ID component part enables the user (or agent) to begin a query with a romanized form and then narrow it down to a specific lexical entry. Moreover, the path to a lemma can be further appended by a hash tag and a number to point to one sense of the lemma.[4] As for URIs of synsets, since a synset typically contains more than one sense and therefore cannot be represented with one single lexical form, CWN uses only IDs to identify a synset, as the RDF version of WordNet does in lemonUby.

While the first two rules address the scheme and the type of URIs to be used, the last two concern the contents to be served when a URL is dereferenced. In adopting the RDF-native *lemon* model,

[1] `http://wordnet-rdf.princeton.edu/`

[2] Note that the same situation is observed with URIs embedded with lexical forms of alphabetic languages when homophony occurs. For example, The URL `http://wordnet-rdf.princeton.edu/wn31/bank-n` points to both "river bank" and "financial bank" in PWN.

[3] `http://lemon-model.net/lexica/uby/wn/`

[4] Fore example, `http://lope.linguistics.ntu.edu.tw/cwn/lod/biao3/041141#11` points to the eleventh sense of the lemma *biao3* "show".

CWN meets the third rule of using standard formats at the outset. As for the fourth rule that requires the inclusion of other URIs, links to PWN's synsets are included that correspond to those of CWN. This last rule is to be addressed in more detail in Section 4.

3.3 CWN as Linked Data

Chief among the threads of information to be converted in RDF are the word senses and synsets of CWN. While the former correspond readily to *lemon*'s lexical senses, their lemmas to *lemon*'s lexical entries, the latter require special treatment. To comply with the aforementioned principle of separating linguistic realizations from underlying concepts, synsets are regarded as ontological references with which word senses are associated. Using the WordNet RDF ontology[5] introduced by McCrae et al.(2014) for use in the context of *lemon*, we represent CWN's synsets as a subclass of *Concept* in SKOS (Miles and Pérez-Agüera, 2007), expressing synsets without describing them with a formal ontological type. Figure 2 depicts a *lemon* representation of the first sense of the lemma *dong4wu4* "animal" in Turtle format.[6]

```
@prefix owl: <http://www.w3.org/2002/07/
    ↪ owl#> .
@prefix rdf: <http://www.w3.org
    ↪ /1999/02/22-rdf-syntax-ns#> .
@prefix lemon: <http://www.lemon-model.
    ↪ net/lemon#> .
@prefix wordnet-ontology: <http://
    ↪ wordnet-rdf.princeton.edu/
    ↪ ontology#> .
<http://lope.linguistics.ntu.edu.tw/cwn/
    ↪ lod/dong4wu4/052268> a lemon:
    ↪ LexicalEntry ;
    lemon:canonicalForm <#CanonicalForm>
        ↪ ;
    lemon:sense <#1> ;
    wordnet-ontology:part_of_speech
        ↪ wordnet-ontology:noun .
<#CanonicalForm> a lemon:Form ;
    lemon:writtenRep          @cmn .
<#1> a lemon:LexicalSense ;
    lemon:reference <http://lope.
        ↪ linguistics.ntu.edu.tw/cwn/
        ↪ lod/2068> ;
    wordnet-ontology:gloss
        ↪
        ↪ @cmn ;
    owl:sameAs <http://wordnet-rdf.
        ↪ princeton.edu/wn31/100015568-
        ↪ n> .
```

Figure 2: The first sense of *dong4wu4* in Turtle.

[5] http://wordnet-rdf.princeton.edu/ontology

[6] http://www.w3.org/TR/turtle/

In the WordNet RDF ontology, however, there is no vocabulary for describing the relation between coordinate terms that share the same classificatory criteria, or *paranymy*. Take *season (of the year)* for example. Except when referring to a tropical climate, a first impression about the term is oftentimes the categorization of *spring*, *summer*, *fall* and *winter*. Other terms such as *dry season* and *rainy season* are not thought of as parallel as the four seasons, even though all of them share the same immediate superordinate concept (Huang et al., 2008). While CWN attends to this syntagmatic relation between different groupings of hyponyms, it can only be expressed when PWN adopts this type of relation or when a tailor-made ontology for *lemon*-CWN is in place.

4 Interlinking *lemon*-CWN on the Web

As shown in Figure 2, there can be an outward link to PWN if the synset referenced by a lexical sense has a comparable entry in PWN. By way of synset mapping, *lemon*-CWN is not only linked to PWN, but also indirectly interlinked with other wordnets via PWN. Besides using PWN as key to the LLOD cloud and interface with other linguistic resources, *lemon*-CWN can be integrated into the Global WordNet Grid when organized, along with other wordnets, by the ontology consisting of 71 Base Types proposed by the Global WordNet Association.[7] An initial mapping has identified 169 synsets comparable to the Base Types.[8]

5 Conclusion

We have described a *lemon*ized version of CWN to be integrated in the LLOD cloud and the Global WordNet Grid. In converting CWN into Linked Data, we have established a URI scheme optimal for encoding Chinese lemmas alternatively written in the Latin alphabet. Also, we have pointed out two aspects of CWN that cannot be expressed using *lemon* and the WordNet RDF ontology, respectively the unit of meaning facets and the relation of paranymy. Future work thus includes finding another model that allows for the representation of meaning facets and designing an ontology for *lemon*-CWN that has vocabulary for paranymy.

[7] http://w.globalwordnet.org/gwa/ewn_to_bc/BaseTypes.htm

[8] http://lope.linguistics.ntu.edu.tw/cwn/gwn/

References

Kathleen Ahrens, Li-Li Chang, Ke-Jiann Chen, and Chu-Ren Huang. 1998. Meaning representation and meaning instantiation for chinese nominals. In *International Journal of Computational Linguistics & Chinese Language Processing, Volume 3, Number 1, February 1998: Special Issue on the 10th Research on Computational Linguistics International Conference*, pages 45–60.

Tim Berners-Lee, James Hendler, and Ora Lassila. 2001. The semantic web. *Scientific American*, 284(5):34–43.

Tim Berners-Lee. 2006. Linked Data. `http://www.w3.org/DesignIssues/LinkedData.html`. [Online; accessed 28-April-2015].

Francis Bond and Ryan Foster. 2013. Linking and extending an open multilingual wordnet. In *ACL (1)*, pages 1352–1362. The Association for Computer Linguistics.

Francis Bond, Christiane Fellbaum, Shu-Kai Hsieh, Chu-Ren Huang, Adam Pease, and Piek Vossen. 2014. A multilingual lexico-semantic database and ontology. In Paul Buitelaar and Philipp Cimiano, editors, *Towards the Multilingual Semantic Web*, pages 243–258. Springer Berlin Heidelberg.

Paul Buitelaar. 2010. Ontology-based semantic lexicons: Mapping between terms and object descriptions. *Ontology and the Lexicon*, pages 212–223.

Catherine Chavula and C. Maria Keet. 2014. Is *lemon* sufficient for building multilingual ontologies for bantu languages? In *Proceedings of the 11th International Workshop on OWL: Experiences and Directions (OWLED 2014) co-located with 13th International Semantic Web Conference on (ISWC 2014), Riva del Garda, Italy, October 17-18, 2014.*, pages 61–72.

Christian Chiarcos, Sebastian Hellmann, and Sebastian Nordhoff. 2011. Towards a linguistic linked open data cloud: The open linguistics working group. *TAL*, pages 245–275.

Gerard De Melo. 2008. Language as a foundation of the semantic web.

Christiane Fellbaum. 1998. *WordNet: An Electronic Lexical Database*. Bradford Books.

Shu-Kai Hsieh. 2011. Sense structure in cube: Lexical semantic representation in chinese wordnet. *International Journal of Computer Processing of Languages*, 23:243–253.

Chu-Ren Huang, Ru-Yng Chang, and Hshiang-Pin Lee. 2004. Sinica bow (bilingual ontological wordnet): Integration of bilingual wordnet and sumo. In *Proceedings of the Fourth International Conference on Language Resources and Evaluation (LREC'04)*. European Language Resources Association (ELRA).

Chu-Ren Huang, I-Li Su, Pei-Yi Hsiao, and Xiu-Ling Ke. 2007. Paranyms, co-hyponyms and antonyms: Representing semantic fields with lexical semantic relations. In *Proceedings of the 8th Chinese Lexical Semantics Workshop 2007*, Hong Kong: Hong Kong Polytechnic University.

Chu-Ren Huang, I-Li Su, Pei-Yi Hsiao, and Xiu-Ling Ke. 2008. Paranymy: Enriching ontological knowledge in wordnets. In *Proceedings of the Fourth Global Wordnet Conference*, pages 221–228, Szeged, Hungary: University of Szeged.

Marek Maziarz, Maciej Piasecki, and Stanisław Szpakowicz. 2013. The chicken-and-egg problem in wordnet design: synonymy, synsets and constitutive relations. *Language Resources and Evaluation*, 47(3):769–796.

John McCrae, Dennis Spohr, and Philipp Cimiano. 2011. Linking lexical resources and ontologies on the semantic web with lemon. In *Proceedings of the 8th Extended Semantic Web Conference on The Semantic Web: Research and Applications - Volume Part I*, ESWC'11, pages 245–259, Berlin, Heidelberg. Springer-Verlag.

John McCrae, Guadalupe Aguado-de Cea, Paul Buitelaar, Philipp Cimiano, Thierry Declerck, Asunción Gómez-Pérez, Jorge Gracia, Laura Hollink, Elena Montiel-Ponsoda, Dennis Spohr, and Tobias Wunner. 2012. Interchanging lexical resources on the semantic web. *Language Resources and Evaluation*, 46(4):701–719.

John P. McCrae, Christiane Fellbaum, and Philipp Cimiano. 2014. Publishing and linking wordnet using lemon and rdf. In *Proceedings of the 3 rd Workshop on Linked Data in Linguistics*.

Alistair Miles and José R. Pérez-Agüera. 2007. Skos: Simple knowledge organisation for the web. *Cataloging & Classification Quarterly*, 43(3):69–83.

Jorge Morato, Miguel Angel Marzal, Juan Lloréns, and José Moreiro. 2004. Wordnet applications. *GLOBAL WORDNET CONFERENCE*, 2:270–278.

Adam Pease, Christiane Fellbaum, and Piek Vossen. 2008. Building the global wordnet grid. *Proceedings of the CIL-18 Workshop on Linguistic Studies of Ontology*.

Author Index